INST

NORW

by Dorothy Thomas and Barbara Robøle

Illustrated by DRAGONFLY DESIGNS

dot publications

Dorothy Thomas first encountered Norway at Girl Guide camp on an island near Stavanger. Since then she has travelled the length and breadth (a whole ten kilometres at its narrowest) of the country by scooter – and much shorter stretches on skis. She studied at Newcastle upon Tyne and Oslo Universities, is a member of the Institute of Linguists, and works as a teacher and translator.

After a brief sojourn in Hell (near Trondheim), **Barbara Robøle** now writes newspaper articles and short stories. When in need of a quiet life (or to escape from her eleven grandchildren), she tends her garden just below the tree-line in Jotunheimen.

First published 1993
Copyright © DM Thomas & BA Robøle 1993

Published by dot Publications
54A Haig Avenue, Whitley Bay, NE25 8JD, Great Britain

ISBN 1 871086 08 6

Production by Roger Booth Associates, Newcastle upon Tyne
Printed in the U.K. by Bell & Bain Ltd., Glasgow

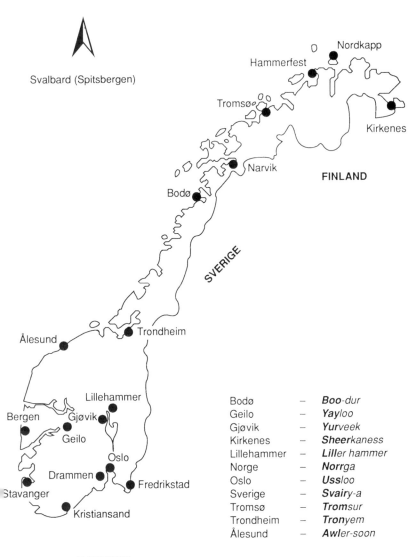

Bodø	–	*Boo-dur*
Geilo	–	*Yayloo*
Gjøvik	–	*Yurveek*
Kirkenes	–	*Sheerkaness*
Lillehammer	–	*Liller hammer*
Norge	–	*Norrga*
Oslo	–	*Ussloo*
Sverige	–	*Svairy-a*
Tromsø	–	*Tromsur*
Trondheim	–	*Tronyem*
Ålesund	–	*Awler-soon*

■4 *Contents*

Introduction

Norwegian and English have many words in common since both are Germanic languages. Norwegian has even closer links with Swedish and Danish and speakers of one can understand the others quite easily. However, for historical and geographical reasons Norwegian is the most fluid language in Europe. For several hundred years until 1814 it was ruled by Denmark, which had a profound influence on the language of the towns, *Bokmål*, while in the country difficulties of access meant that a variety of accents developed, which were later synthesised into *Nynorsk*. In this book we have used a fairly neutral form of *Bokmål* which is used by most newspapers and magazines and will be understood everywhere.

Since everyone has the right not only to speak his dialect but to write it, a word may have several, usually minor, variations. Bm *en* is often Nn *ei (en/ein – ne)*, Bm *u* = Nn *o (hull/hol* – hole), Bm *h* = Nn *k (hvit/kvit* – white), Bm *å* = Nn *a (hånd/hand* – hand); Nn often adds a *j (ikke/ikkje* – not). Other common variations are *jeg/eg* (I), *kirke/kyrkje* (church), *melk/mjølk* (milk). *Syv/sju* (7), *tyve/tjue* (20), *frem/fram* (forward), *syk/sjuk* (sick), *vann/vatn* (lake) and *vei/veg* (way) also coexist.

Bokmål has two genders, common and neuter, while *Nynorsk* has a feminine gender too. Among those words which frequently use the feminine version are *boka/boken* (the book), *klokka/klokken* (o'clock), *kona/konen* (the wife), *kua/kuen* (the cow), *stua/stuen* (the living room).

Using this book. Inside the back cover is a list of basic phrases which you can use in a variety of circumstances. First look up what you need in the Contents section or the Index, then follow the speech guides beneath each picture. The guide on page 8 will help you pronounce it correctly. The syllables you should stress are set in heavy type.

Next we take you through a series of typical situations, giving you the words you'll need to get what you want, and some of the likely replies. In most cases we give you a basic situation which can be used in several places. For example, the phrases used in the baker's on page 28 can be used in most other shops too. Sentences are carefully designed to be interchangeable, so that if you want something different from what is being asked for in the picture, you can just slot it in.

In the Index you will sometimes find words included that are related to the one you are actually looking under. For example, under 'Nice' you will also find page 71 where 'Delicious' is used.

Right at the back on page 80 is a list of numbers. Do try to learn these – numbers are a vital part of any language and will make shopping and making arrangements very much easier.

Remember, travelling abroad should be fun. If you can talk to people and understand most of the signs you'll enjoy it much more. Don't be shy – have a go!

Enjoy yourself and have a good trip. – ***God fornøyelse og god tur!***

Things: Nouns. In Norwegian all nouns are thought of as being either common gender (c.: masculine and feminine combined) or neuter gender (n.).

[The language is constantly evolving and some words are frequently used with the feminine article (*ei* = a, *-a* = the), but this is not obligatory and the common articles (*en* = a, *-en* = the) may also be used.]

When talking about one thing only, i.e. a **singular** item (s.), **a** is *en* (c.) or *et* (n.). For **the**, put *en* (c.) or *et* (n.) on the end of the word,

e.g.   *en katt* (c.) – a cat   *katten* – the cat
       et vindu (n.) – a window   *vinduet* – the window
(Note that when *-et* means 'the', *-t* is not pronounced: 'vin-doo-a'.)

If there is more than one, i.e. **plural**, add *-er* for all genders,
e.g.   *katter* – cats   *vinduer* – windows
Monosyllabic neuter nouns, however, do not change in the plural,
e.g.   *et hus* – a house, *flere hus* – several houses.

For **the** in the plural, put *ene* on the end of the original word,
e.g.   *kattene* – the cats   *vinduene* – the windows

Describing things: Adjectives.
If a noun is common gender, the adjective describing it will be too. If a noun is neuter, or there is more than one, the ending of the adjective changes slightly,
e.g.   *en stor katt* – a big cat   *et stort vindu* – a big window
       store katter – big cats   *store vinduer* – big windows

Just to confuse the issue, if you want to say 'the big cat' etc., you have to add an extra 'the' and use the plural form of the adjective.
Thus: *den store katten* – the big cat   *det store vinduet* – the big window
       de store kattene – the big cats   *de store vinduene* – the big windows
(Again, *-t* is not pronounced: 'day stora vin-doo-a'.)

Little/small is the most complicated adjective:
en liten, et lite – a little; *den, det lille* – the little (sing.); *de små-* the small (pl.)

It's mine: Possessive adjectives.
The word for 'my', 'your', etc. depends on whether the **following** word is common, neuter or in the plural, e.g. *min katt* – my cat, *mine katter* – my cats, *mitt hus* – my house, *mine hus* – my houses. (*Katten min, kattene mine* also mean 'my cat', 'my cats'.)

	c.	n.	pl.		c.	n.	pl.
my	*min*	*mitt*	*mine*	our	*vår*	*vårt*	*våre*
your (s.)	*din*	*ditt*	*dine*	your (pl.)	*deres*	*deres*	*deres*
his	*hans*	*hans*	*hans*	their	*deres*	*deres*	*deres*
hers	*hennes*	*hennes*	*hennes*	or their*	*sine*	*sine*	*sine*
or his/hers*	*sin*	*sitt*	*sine*				

*The forms *sin, sitt, sine* are part of the object, so they can only be used when referring to something that has already been mentioned in a particular sentence. They are never part of the subject of a sentence and very rarely occur at the beginning of one. *Sin, sitt,* etc. often mean the same as 'own' in English, e.g. *han kjører sin bil* – he is driving his (own) car, whereas *hans* means it belongs to someone else, e.g. *han kjører hans (Pers) bil* – he is driving his (Per's) car.]

Doing things: Verbs.

These are always the same, regardless of who is doing the action. *(De, Deres* are the formal forms of 'you, your' now mostly replaced by *du, din/ditt/dine*.)

to come	*å komme*	to see	*å se*
I come	*jeg kommer*	I see	*jeg ser*
you come (s.)	*du kommer*	you see (s.)	*du ser*
he, she comes	*han, hun kommer*	he, she sees	*han, hun ser*
it comes (c./n.)	*den, det kommer*	it sees (c./n.)	*den, det ser*
we come	*vi kommer*	we see	*vi ser*
you come (pl.)	*dere kommer*	you see (pl.)	*dere ser*
they come	*de kommer*	they see	*de ser*

to be	*å være*	to have	*å ha*
I am	*jeg er*	I have	*jeg har*
you are (s.)	*du er*	you have (s.)	*du har*
he, she is	*han, hun er*	he, she has	*han, hun har*
it is (c./n.)	*den, det er*	it has (c./n.)	*den, det har*
we are	*vi er*	we have	*vi har*
you are (pl.)	*dere er*	you have (pl.)	*dere har*
they are	*de er*	they have	*de har*

to be able	*å kunne*	to have to	*å måtte*
I can	*jeg kan*	I must	*jeg må* (no r)

to go: use *skal* with no extra verb, e.g. *jeg skal til Norge* – I shall go to Norway, *hun skal til byen* – she will go into town. (Use *skal* for each person.) For the future tense use *skal* with the infinitive,
e.g.   *han skal komme* – he will come, *de skal spise* – they will eat.

to want: for 'I would like' use *jeg vil gjerne* plus the infinitive, e.g. *jeg vil gjerne komme til Norge* – I would like to come to Norway. Again, use *vil* for each person.

Questions: simply take the basic statement and turn it round,
e.g.   *du snakker engelsk* – you speak English
       snakker du engelsk? – do you speak English?

Saying No: *ikke* = not. It usually comes after the first part of the verb,
e.g.   *jeg snakker ikke norsk* – I don't speak Norwegian
       jeg kan ikke snakke norsk – I can't speak Norwegian.

8 *Sounds*

We have tried to keep our transcription as simple as possible so that you can read the questions and answers almost as if they were English. Some words are split by a hyphen to make them easier to read and to get the stress in the right place. Double consonants are both pronounced, like k in bank card or t in boat trip.

a when short is very close to **o** in on; long like **a** in father.
e short like **e** in met; when long, like **air** but without the **r**.
i short, as in bit; when long, like **ee** in bee.
o usually **oo** as in moon. It can also be a short sound – *bok/book* sound alike.
  Sometimes it resembles **aw** in paw, or **o** in hot.
u is the Scots or French **u**, or German **ü**. Sometimes like **oo** in book.
y similar to short **u**. Make as if to say **ee**, then round your lips and push them forward.
æ is an open sound, like **ai** in air.
ø is like **ur** in fur (without the r) or **uh** in uh-huh.
å as in paw, or **o** in hot.
au is like a short **e** as in met, followed by **oo**. (It also means Ow!)
ei like **ay** in say.
øy is like **uh** followed by **ee**.

g as in go.
gei, gi, gj, gy, like **y** in yes.
j, hj, lj, like **y** in yes.
k as in kid.
ki, kj, ky is the German **ch** as in ich. In English it is the **h** sound as in human, huge.
ng as in singer, never as in finger.
r is lightly rolled; the southwest uses a French **r**, produced in the throat.
rs is often pronounced **sh**, expecially in the east.
s,z always like **s** in sit, never a **z** sound.
sj, skj pronounced **sh** as in she.
sk like **sk** in skate, but **sk** with i, y, øy is pronounced **sh**.

Silent consonants
d in the combinations **ld, nd, rd**. Usually silent after a long vowel, e.g. *god, rød.*
g as in **ig, lig**.
h before **j, v,** e.g. *hjem, hva.*
t when in 'the' e.g. *huset* (the house), or in *det* (it). Always pronounced in the past tense of verbs, e.g. *stoppet* (stopped).
v in *halv* (half), *selv* (self), *sølv* (silver), *tolv* (twelve).

Intonation
Like Swedish, Norwegian has two speech melodies or tones which are used in combination with stress and to differentiate between some words, but these tones are not shown in our transcription.

Long words
Since these are often several words combined, try splitting them after an *s* or an *e*.

Time of Day and Greetings

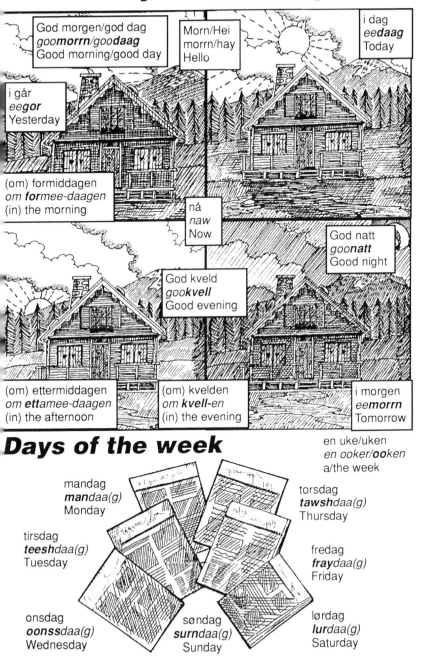

God morgen/god dag
goomorrn/goodaag
Good morning/good day

Morn/Hei
morrn/hay
Hello

i dag
eedaag
Today

i går
eegor
Yesterday

(om) formiddagen
om formee-daagen
(in) the morning

nå
naw
Now

God natt
goonatt
Good night

God kveld
gookvell
Good evening

(om) ettermiddagen
om ettamee-daagen
(in) the afternoon

(om) kvelden
om kvell-en
(in) the evening

i morgen
eemorrn
Tomorrow

Days of the week

en uke/uken
en ooker/ooken
a/the week

mandag
mandaa(g)
Monday

torsdag
tawshdaa(g)
Thursday

tirsdag
teeshdaa(g)
Tuesday

fredag
fraydaa(g)
Friday

onsdag
oonssdaa(g)
Wednesday

søndag
surndaa(g)
Sunday

lørdag
lurdaa(g)
Saturday

Hotels

In ascending order of price you'll find **hotell, turisthotell** and in the mountains **høyfjellshotell**, and the cost will include a large buffet-style breakfast. A boarding house (**pensjonat, hospits, gjestgiveri** or **turisthytte**) will be less ruinous but may only provide breakfast – and charge extra for it. If you have sleeping bags you might like to rent a **hytte** or cabin (you may also need pans and crockery). Alternatively, look for a private room (**rom, værelse, overnatting**). **Ledig** means vacant, **til leie** is to let, and one **med kjøkken** has cooking facilities.

If you've booked

1. God dag.
2. God dag.
3. Jeg har bestilt et rom. Navnet er Jones.
4. Det stemmer. Kan jeg få passet? Skriv under her.

RESEPSJON

1. *Goodaag.*
   Hello.

2. *Goodaag.*
   Hello.

3. *Yay har bestilt ett room. Naavner air Jones.*
   I have booked a room in the name of Jones.

4. *Day stem-mer. Kanyay faw passer? Skreev oon-ner hair.*
   Of course. May I have your passport? Could you sign here, please?

Meals:

frokost	lunsj	middag
frookost	*lunsh*	*mid-daa(g)*
breakfast	lunch	dinner

helpensjon/halvpensjon *hail/hal pen-shoon* full/half board

LIFT (heisen): Press *HIT* to summon.

This sign is for the Tourist Office (**Turistinformasjon**), all of whom speak English. They will often find you a hotel or private room for a small charge (look for **Innkvartering** or **Romformidling**) and can also make travel reservations.

1. *Goo**daag**. **Har**doo ett room for natt'n?*
   Hello. Have you a room available?

2. *Yaa, vor **mang**-er **bleer** day?*
   Yes, how many for?

3. *For ain/too pe**shoon**(er) oh ett (too) **barn**.*
   For one/two people and one child (two children).

4. *Got. Vor **mang**-er **net**-ter?*
   Fine. For how many nights?

5. *For **ain** natt (en **ooker**).*
   For one night (a week).

1. *__Skal__day __vair__er __dob__-belt __el__-ler __eng__-kelt room?*
   Would you like a double room or a single?

2. *Ett **dob**-belt oh too **eng**-kelt room.*
   A double and two singles.

3. *__May__ el-ler __oot__'n doosh?*
   With shower or without?

4. *May doosh.*
   With shower.

1. *Yaa, day **finss** ett room **lay**dee.*
   Yes, we have a room available.

2. *Vor **mee**-er **cost**er day?*
   How much is it?

3. *Day bleer — **kroon**er natt'n.*
   It's — kroner a night.

4. *Braa. Yay **tar** day.*
   Fine. I'll take it.

5. *Air **froo**kost inklu-**dairt**?*
   Is breakfast included?

6. *Vor **kan**yay par-**kair**er?*
   Where can I park?

1. *Got. Va var **naav**ner?*
   Good. What is your name, please?

2. *Yay **hay**ter Helen Baker.*
   My name is Baker.

3. ***Kan**yay faw **pas**-ser **day**ress, tak?*
   Could I have your passport, please?

4. ***Mang**-er tak. Hair air **nur**klen.*
   Thank you. Here is your key.

★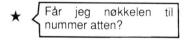

*Fawyay **nur**klen til **noom**-mer att'n?*
May I have the key to room 18, please?

1. Får jeg se på rommet?
2. Ja, selvfølgelig.
3. Fint, jeg tar det.
4. Nei takk, det passer ikke. Det er for bråkete (lite).
5. Finnes det noe bedre?
6. Jeg beklager ...

1. **Faw**yay sair paw room-mer?
   Can I see the room?
2. Yaa, sell-**fur**ga-lee.
   Yes, of course.
3. Feent, yay tar day.
   Good, I'll take it.
4. Nay tak, day **pas**-ser ik-ker. Day air for **braw**ker-ta (**lee**ter).
   No, I don't like it. It's too noisy (small).
5. Finns day noo-er **bay**drer?
   Have you anything better?
6. Yay be**klaag**er ...
   I'm sorry ...

Hotel meals

1. Serverer dere mat her?
2. Når serverer dere frokost? (lunsj, middag)
3. Fra klokka halv åtte.

Checking out

1. Kan jeg få regningen, takk.
2. Takk for nå!

1. Sair-**vair**er dayrer maat hair?
   Do you serve meals here?
2. Norr sair-**vair**er dayrer **froo**kost? (lunsh/**mid**-daag)
   What time do you serve breakfast? (lunch/dinner)
3. Fra **klok**-ker hal **ot**-ter.
   From 7.30.

1. **Kan**yay faw **rain**ing-en, tak.
   Please may I have the bill.
2. Tak for naw!
   Goodbye.

(Time p.74, Paying p.35)

You will usually know your host's name, so just ask:

Finding your apartment or cabin

1. Unnskyld, kan du si meg hvor Herr — bor? OR
2. Jeg ser etter Fru —.

1. **Oon-**shull, **kan**doo see may vor Hair — **boor?**
   Excuse me, where does Mr — live?

2. Yay sair et-ter Fruw —.
   I'm looking for Mrs —.

På hytta – *paw hit-ta* – **At the cabin**
Kjøkkenet   **shukk**er-na   the Kitchen

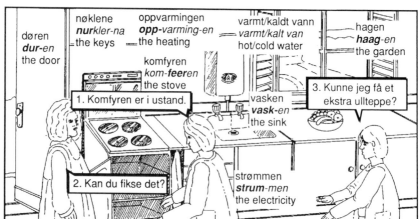

døren
dur-en
the door

nøklene
nurkler-na
the keys

oppvarmingen
opp-varming-en
the heating

komfyren
kom-feeren
the stove

1. Komfyren er i ustand.

2. Kan du fikse det?

varmt/kaldt vann
varmt/kalt van
hot/cold water

hagen
haag-en
the garden

vasken
vask-en
the sink

strømmen
strum-men
the electricity

3. Kunne jeg få et ekstra ullteppe?

1. **Kom-feeren** air ee **oo-**stan.
   The stove isn't working/is broken.

2. **Kan**doo **fix**er day?
   Can you mend it?

3. **Koon-**ner yay faw ett extra **ool-**tepper?
   Could I have (another blanket), please?

Soverommet	gardinener	lyset	en lyspære	Badet
sover-roommer	*gardeener-na*	*lees-ser*	*en leess-pairer*	*baader*
The Bedroom	the curtains	the light	a light bulb	**The Bathroom**

W.C./Toalettet
vaysay/twa-letter
the Lavatory/Toilet

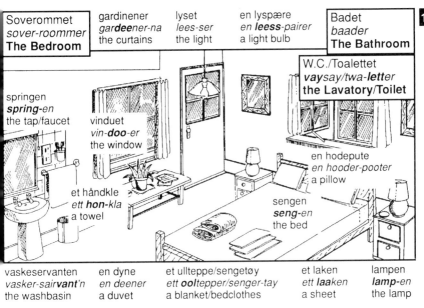

springen
spring-en
the tap/faucet

vinduet
vin-doo-er
the window

et håndkle
ett hon-kla
a towel

en hodepute
en hooder-pooter
a pillow

sengen
seng-en
the bed

vaskeservanten	en dyne	et ullteppe/sengetøy	et laken	lampen
vasker-sairvant'n	*en deener*	*ett oolltepper/senger-tay*	*ett laaken*	*lamp-en*
the washbasin	a duvet	a blanket/bedclothes	a sheet	the lamp

en kopp/et krus	et glass	en tallerken
en kopp/ett krooss	*ett glass*	*en ta-lairken*
a cup/mug	a glass	a plate

en kasserolle
en kasser-rol-er
a saucepan

en stekepanne
en stayker-panner
a frying pan

søppelen	kjøleskapet	en gaffel	en kniv	en bolle	en mugge
sur-plen	*shurler-skaaper*	*en gaff-ell*	*en k(a)-neev*	*en boller*	*en mugger*
the rubbish/trash	the fridge	a fork	a knife	a bowl	a jug

et tørkehåndkle	en stol	en skje/teskje	kaffe/tekannen	bordet
ett turker-honkler	*en stool*	*en shay/tay-shay*	*kaffer/taykannen*	*boorer*
a tea-towel	a chair	a spoon/teaspoon	the coffee/teapot	the table

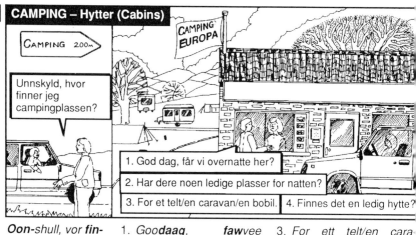

Oon-shull, vor **fin**-ner yay **camp**ing **plas**sen?
Excuse me, where is the campsite?

1. *Goo**daag**, **faw**vee **awv**er-**natt**er hair?*
   Hello, can we camp here?

2. *Har dayrer **noo**-en **lay**dy-er **plas**-ser for natt'n?*
   Have you any room tonight?

3. *For ett telt/en caravan/en **boo**-beel.*
   For a tent/caravan/ motor caravan.

4. *Finss day en **lay**dy hitter?*
   Is there a cabin available?

Campsite signs

Bommen Stengt
23.00-07.00
Barrier closed
11p.m.-7a.m.

Toalett Toilet
Kjøkken Kitchen
Vaskerom Laundry

Tømming av toalett bøtter
Chemical toilet disposal point

1. *Vor mang-er bleer dayrer?*
   How many are there of you?

3. *Vor lenger har dayrer tenkt aw **blee**?*
   How long would you like to stay?

2. *Baarer ain./Too voxner oh ett (too barn).*
   Just one./Two adults and one child (two children).

4. *Ain natt (to net-ter/en ooker).*
   One night (two nights/a week).

1. *Helst may strurm, tak.*
   I'd like electricity, too.

2. *Hva air preessen pair dayn?*
   How much is it per night?

4. *Norr steng-er dayrer om kvell-en?*
   What time do you close in the evening?

3. *Day bleer — krona.*
   That will be — kroner.

5. *Klokker elver.*
   At eleven o'clock.

* Small blue gas cartridges are sold in Scandinavia but not large gas bottles since butane freezes at very low temperatures: propane is used instead.

* Camping is allowed anywhere on open land provided you are at least 150m away from houses or cabins (ask permission if possible). No fires are allowed in woodland from April 15th-September 15th.

* **Camping ikke tillatt/forbud**t – No Camping

Youth Hostel/Mountain Hut

Vandrerhjemmet	Fjellstuen
vandrer-yemmer	*f-yell stoo-en*
the Youth Hostel	the Mountain Hut

Bestyreren
besteerer-en
the Warden

1. *Goodaag, har dayrer noo-er laydy?*
   Hallo, have you any room?

3. *Hair air medlemss-korter mit.*
   Here's my membership card.

2. *Vor leng-er har doo tenkt aw blee?*
   How long for?

4. *Har doo may laaken-poosser (sover-poosser)?*
   Have you a sheet bag (sleeping bag)?

SNACKS (p.20): you can get these at a **Kiosk** or **Snackbar**, or coffee, cakes and **smørbrød** (open sandwiches) at a **Konditori** *(konditor-ree)*. Everywhere has a **Gatekjøkken** ('street kitchen', p.21) with fast food like **varme pølser** (hot dogs), pieces of pizza and chicken, and soft drinks. For a full meal try a **Kafé** *(kaf-fay)*, **Kafeteria**, **Kaffistova** or anywhere with **-stua** in its name. All are self-service and there's one in most department stores, supermarkets and large stations. Other places to look for are **Kro** *(kroo)*, **Restaurant**, **Veikro** or **Vertshus**. (**Hjemme-laget mat** means 'home-cooking' and **Servering** *(sair-vairing)* is 'refreshments'.)

USEFUL TERMS: **Dagens rett** – day's special
Koldtbord – cold buffet
Lunsjbord – lunchtime buffet, includes some hot dishes
'Stor eller liten?' – 'large or small?'

TIPPING? Service is included in the bill. Norwegians don't tip. Ever.

MEALS: frokost *(frookost)* breakfast; lunsj *(lunsh)* lunch; middag *(mid-daag)* dinner. Breakfast is a massive buffet of cold meat/cold cuts, cheese and fish.

Except at restaurants, you will get most choice at lunchtime when the day's special and other hot dishes are served well into the afternoon. (Between 11.30am and 1pm office workers invade the cafés for snacks to tide them over until dinner at home at 5 or 6pm.) Self-service establishments are usually closed by about 6 pm.

DRINKS: Coffee (p.19) is served strong and black. Tea is normally black, often with lemon – you will have to ask for milk ('te med melk'). Norwegians often drink plain water, fruit squash or milk with their meals.

You can get a beer (p.19) or a glass of wine (pp.19; 26) at most bars and open-air cafés, as well as at hotels and restaurants. Beer and wine are served all day, but spirits are only available 1-11pm and never on Sundays. Supermarkets sell beer at about half bar prices ('pant' – 'deposit'). Wine (reasonable in price) and spirits (prohibitive) are only sold at state-controlled shops, **Vinmonopolet**, known as 'Polet' *(pooler)* so use your duty-free allowance – one litre of each of wine and spirits for all aged twenty or over.

In much of the west no alcohol is available at all except for 'lettøl' (non-alcoholic lager) and Vørterøl, a sweet version.

Do not drink if driving – the regulations are very strictly enforced.

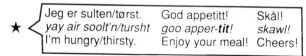

★	Jeg er sulten/tørst.	God appetitt!	Skål!
	yay air soolt'n/tursht	*goo apper-**tit**!*	*skawl!*
	I'm hungry/thirsty.	Enjoy your meal!	Cheers!

en lettøl
*en **let** url*
a low-alcohol beer

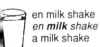

en fatøl
*en **faat** url*
a draught beer

en milk shake
*en **milk** shake*
a milk shake

en cola
*en **cooler***
a coke

appelsinsaft
*appel-**seen** saft*
orange juice

en sitronbrus
*en sit-**roon** brooss*
a fizzy lemonade

en kopp sjokolade
*en kop shokko-**laad**er*
a hot chocolate

en te (med melk/sitron)
*en tay (may melk/si-**troon**)*
a tea (with milk/lemon)

to kaffe (med sukker)
*to **kaf**-fer (may **sook**-ker)*
two coffees (with sugar)

---

2. Serverer dere øl eller vin?

4. Kan jeg få en kaffe, te (med melk), en pils og et glass eplesaft.

1. God dag. Hva skal det være?

3. Ja, begge deler.

1. *Goo**daag**. Va skal day **vair**er?*
   Hello, what would you like?

2. *Sair-**vairer** dayrer url el-ler **veen**?*
   Do you serve beer or wine?

3. *Yaa, **beg**-ger **day**ler.*
   Yes, both.

4. ***Kan**yay faw en **kaf**-fer, tay (may melk), en pilss oh ett glass **epl**er-saft.*
   Can have a coffee, a tea (with milk), a lager and a glass of apple juice.

Paying, finding the lavatory

1. Er det ledig her?

2. Tusen takk. Hvor mye blir det?

3. Unnskyld, hvor er toalettene?

1. *Air day **lay**dy hair?*
   Is this seat/table free?

2. ***Too**ssen tak. Vor **mee**-er **bleer** day?*
   Thank you. How much is that?

3. ***Oon**-shull, vor air twa-**lett**erna?*
   Excuse me, where are the toilets?

1. *Va slaags **smur**brur har **day**rer?*
   What open sandwiches have you got?

2. *Vee har **oost**er-**smur**brur, **shin**ker **smur**brur, may **egg** oh may **ray**ker.*
   We have cheese smørbrød, ham smørbrød, egg and shrimp.

3. *En **smoolt**ring oh ett **stik**-ker eple **kaak**er.*
   A doughnut and a slice of apple cake.

4. *Det-ter **hair**.*
   This one.

Self-service/Choosing things

bløtkake
blurt-kaaker
cream gateau

vafler
vaffler
waffles

et wienerbrød
ett veener-brur
a Danish pastry

Napoleonskake
*napoolay-**onss** kaaker*
vanilla slice

1. *Va air **det**-ter?*
   What's this called?

2. ***Kan**yay faw lit aav **den dair**?*
   Can I have some of that, please.

3. *Vilker **grurn** saaker?*
   Which vegetables?

4. ***Deess**er oh **dee dair**.*
   These and those.

Fast Food – *Gatekjøkken* (gaater *shuk*-ken)

ARME PØLSER – *varmer purlser* – hot dogs

★ en pølse, takk
en purlser, tak
a hot dog, please

et rundstykke med ost
*ett **roon**-stikker may oost*
a cheese roll (half)

en pizza
en peetser
a pizza

pommes frites
pom free
chips/fries

potetgull
*poo-**tayt**gool*
crisps/chips

en grillpølse
*en **grill** purlser*
a thick, grilled frankfurter

med brød/lompe
*may brur/**lumper***
in a roll/potato cake

med sennep og ketchup
*may **sennep** oh **ket**chup*
with mustard & tomato sauce

Is – *eess* – Ice cream

en kuleis
*en **cool**er eess*
a cone

en softis
en soft eess
a soft ice

en saftis
en saft eess
an ice lolly

krokan
*kroo-**kaan***
roasted nuts

1. *Har dayrer **eess** krem?*
   Have you any ice cream?

2. *Yaa, va-**neel**yer, **yoor**bair oh shokko-**laad**er.*
   Yes, vanilla, strawberry and chocolate.

3. *En shokko-**laad**er eess.*
   A chocolate ice cream.

4. *Stoor ella leet'n? Ain **cool**er **el**-ler too?*
   Large or small? One scoop or two?

5. *En sleek.*
   One like that.

1. *Morrn! Kan yay(vee) faw **froo**kost?*
   Good morning. Could I(we) have breakfast?

4. ***Kan**yay faw lit brur?*
   Could I have some bread, please?

2. *Tay **el**-ler **kaf**-fer?*
   Tea or coffee?

3. *Tay/**kaf**-fer may melk, tak.*
   Tea/coffee with milk, please.

et glass...	ost	fisk	rundstykker/ristet brød
ett glass	*oost*	*fisk*	***roon**-stikker/**ris**tet brur*
a glass of...	cheese	fish	rolls/toast

varm/kald melk
varm/kal melk
hot/cold milk

kjøttpålegg
***shirt**-pawleg*
sliced meat

Restaurants – Booking a table

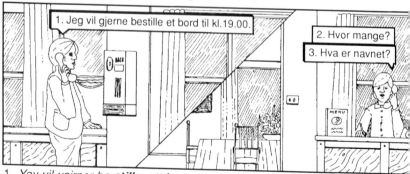

1. *Yay vil yairner be-**still**er ett boor tll klokker **nitt'**n.*
   I'd like to book a table for 7 o'clock.

2. *Vor **mang**-er?*
   How many for?

3. *Va air **naav**ner?*
   What name, please?

Telephone p.41

1. *Goodaag, har dayrer ett boor til tray?*
   Hello, have you a table for three?

2. *Ett ay-er blik... Har dayrer be-stilt?*
   Just a moment ... Have you booked?

Ordering a meal

1. *Va air daag-enss ret?*
   What is today's special?

2. *En/too too-maat sup-per.*
   One/two tomato soups, please.

3. *Yay tar en lammer kotter-let – og T-bone steak til may.*
   I'll have a lamb chop – and T-bone steak for me.

4. *En hamburger may pom free oh sa-laat, tak.*
   I'd like a hamburger with chips and salad.

5. *Skal day vairer des-sair?*
   Would you like dessert?

Sair-vairer dayrer vayghe-tar koost?
   Have you any vegetarian dishes?

★ Serverer dere vegetarkost?

Meny – men-nee – Menu — 1

Long words: often the last part is the item's name and the first part describes it, so try splitting words after an *s* or an *e*. (Each dish has been hyphenated to give you the idea.) There is more meat and fish on p.29, vegetables on p.30.

SUPPE – Soup

Asparges-suppe
*as**par**gass supper*
Asparagus soup

Blomkål-suppe
***bloom**kawl supper*
Cauliflower soup

Erte-suppe
airter supper
Pea soup with ham

Fiske-suppe
fisker supper
Fish soup

Tomat-suppe
*too-**maat** supper*
Tomato soup

EGGRETTER – Egg dishes

Egge-røre
egger-rurer
Scrambled egg

et Speil-egg
ett spayl-egg
a Fried Egg

en Omelett
***oom**er-let*
an Omelette

(med ost/skinke/sopp)
(may oost/shinker/sop)
(cheese/ham/mushroom)

SALATER – Salads

Blandet salat
blann**ɛt sa-**laat
Mixed salad

Reke-salat
*rayker sa-**laat***
Prawn salad

Tun-fisk-salat
toon**fisk sa-**laat
Tuna salad

FISK – Fish

Fiske-grateng
*fisker **graa**teng*
Fish, macaroni, cheese, breadcrumbs

Grav-/Røke-laks
graav-lax/rurker-lax
Cured/Smoked Salmon

Sur-Sild
Soor sil
Salted herring, pepper & onions

Sei-biff
say biff
Fried Coley

Stekt Ørret
*stekt **ur**-rett*
Fried Trout

Rødspette
rur spetter
Plaice

Panert Torsk
*pa-**nairt** torshk*
Breaded Cod

Benløse fugler
baynlurser fooler
Beef olives

Biff med løk
biff may lurk
Beef and onions

Fenalår
fayner-lor
Cured leg of Mutton

Hønse-frikassé
hurnser frikker-say
Fricassée of Chicken

Karbonader
karbo-naader
Beefburgers

Kjøtt-gryte
shirt greeter
Meat stew

Kjøtt-kaker
shirt kaaker
Meat balls

1/2 Kylling
hal shilling
1/2 Roast Chicken

brun/lys Lapskaus
lap-skowss
Beef/Pork & potato stew

Mørbrad-biff
murbraar biff
Beef sirloin

Nakke-kotelett
nakker kotter-let
Lamb cutlet

Okse-filét
okser fee-lay
Fillet of Beef

Pinne-kjøtt
pinner shirt
Salted rib of Mutton

Reins-dyr-stek
rains-deer steak
Roast Deer

Ribbe
ribber
Roast rib of Pork

Røkte pølser
rurkter purlser
Smoked Sausages

Schnitzel
shnitsel
Escalope

Speke-mat
spayker maat
Cured sliced Meat

Svine-kam
sveener-kam
Roast saddle of Pork

Svine-kotelett
sveener kotter-let
Pork chop

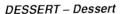

DESSERT – Dessert

Eple-kake
epler kaaker
Apple cake

Is, is-kake
eess kaaker
Ice cream/layer cake

Karamell-pudding
Karra-mel pud-ding
Cream caramel

Ris-grøt
Reess grurt
Rice pudding

Multer
Moolter
Cloudberries

Rømme-grøt
Rum-mer grurt
Wheat flour & sour cream

Tilslørte bondepiker
Tilslurter boonner peeker
Layered apple, sugar, crumbs & cream

1. *Skal day **vair**rer noo-er aw drik-ker?*
   Would you like anything to drink?

2. *En **flask**er **rur**-veen (**veet-**/ **rossay-**/**moossairer-na** veen), tak.*
   A bottle of red wine (white/rosé/sparkling wine), please.

3. *En url, en **mugg**er van oh en **app**el**seen** juice.*
   A beer, a jug of water and an orange juice, please.

Requests and paying

1. ***Kan**yay faw en extra shay?*
   Could I have another spoon, please?

2. *S**maak**ter day?*
   Did you enjoy it?

3. *Tak, day var **day**ly.*
   It was very nice, thank you.

4. ***Kan**yay faw **rain**ing-en,tak?*
   Could I have the bill, please?

5. *Yay troor day air fail ee **rain**ing-en.*
   I think there's a mistake in the bill.

Cutlery, etc. p.15

Shopping

ÅPEN   LUKKET/STENGT
Open   Closed

Opening times: Normal hours are 9am – 5pm Monday to Friday, later on Thursdays and 2 or 3pm on Saturdays. Kiosks and takeaway food stalls stay open in the evening until 10 or 11 pm, as well as at weekends.
Besides the supermarket (**supermarked**) or the market place (**torget**), you will also find small food shops signed **Dagligvarer, Kolonial, Landhandel** or **Matvarer**. Petrol stations often keep food, too.

How to ask:

Har du (epler)?
*har doo (**ep**ler)?*
Have you (any apples)?

Hva koster det/de?
*va **cost**er day/dee?*
How much is it/are they?

Kan jeg få (noen epler)?
kanyay faw (**noo**-en **ep**ler)?
Can I have (some apples), please?

En kilo (tomater)
*en sheelo (too-**maat**er)*
A kilo (of tomatoes)

Hvor mange/mye?
*vor **mang**-er/**mee**-er?*
How much/many?

Én/to
ain /too
One/two

Den/de der
den/dee dair
That one/those

Én skive/to skiver
*ain sheever/**too** sheever*
One slice/two slices (of)

Et stykke
*ett **stik**-ker*
One piece (of)

Halvparten
hal part'n
Half

En kvart/halv kilo
*en k-**vart**/**hal** sheelo*
250/500g ($^1/_2$lb/1lb)

En hekto
*en **hek**too*
100g ($3^1/_2$oz)

En (halv) liter
en (hal) leeter
A (half) litre ($^3/_4$ / $1^3/_4$pts)

Nok?
nok?
Is that enough?

Litt til.
*lit **til***
A little more.

Nok!
nok!
That's enough.

(Nei) dessverre.
*(nay) dess-**verr**er*
Sorry, we haven't any.

Jeg bare ser.
*yay **baar**er **sair***
I'm just looking.

Skal det være noe annet?
*skal day **vair**er **noo**-er **aant**?*
Would you like anything else?

Stykket
Each

Tilbud
Special offer

Hjemmebakt/laget
Home-baked/made

Note: Use the conversation pattern shown in the baker's for all kinds of shops. Remember to say 'Morn' going in, and 'Ha det' or 'Morn'a' when you leave.

boller
bol-ler
sweet buns

flat/knekkebrød
*flaat/k-**nekk**er brur*
crispbread

et kneip
*ett k-**nape***
a brown loaf

en loff
*en **looff***
a white loaf

et helkornbrød
*ett **haylkorn** brur*
a wholemeal

1. *Morrn.*
   Good morning.

2. *Morrn. **Va** vil doo **haa**?*
   Good morning. What would you like?

3. *Yay skal haa ett **brur**. Ett **stoort** brur/ett **leet**er brur. **Det**-ter.*
   I'd like some bread. A large loaf/a small loaf. That one.

1. *Oh **noo**-en **roon** stik-ker. **Too**, tak.*
   And some (crisp) rolls. Two, please.

2. *Vair saw **goo**. Air day **alt**?*
   There you are. Is that everything?

3. *Tak, day **klaar**er say. Vor **mee**-er **bleer** day?*
   No, that's all. How much is that

4. *Day bleer — **kroon**er til-**sam**-men.*
   That's — kroner altogether.

5. *Vair saw **goo**.*
   Here you are.

6. ***Too**ssen tak. Mor-**na**!*
   Thank you. Goodbye.

Kjøtt – *shirt* – Meat

KALKUN
*kal-**koon***
Turkey

KALVEKJØTT
kalver *shirt*
Veal

KJØTTDEIG
shirt dayg
Mince

en KOTELETT
*en kotter-**let***
a Chop/Cutlet

en KYLLING
*en **shil**-ling*
a Chicken

LAMMEKJØTT
***lam**-mer shirt*
Lamb

LEVER/-POSTEI
lay**ver/-pos**stay
Liver/-paté

OKSEKJØTT
***ox**er shirt*
Beef

PØLSER
***purl**ser*
Sausages

RENSDYR
***rayn**ss deer*
Venison

(speke)SKINKE
***spayk**er **shink**er*
(cured, smoked)
Ham

SVINEKJØTT
***svee**ner shirt*
Pork

Fisk – Skalldyr: *fisk – skal deer*: Fish – Seafood

BLÅSKJELL
***blaw** shell*
Mussels

FISKEBOLLER
***fisk**er **bol**-ler*
Fishballs

en HUMMER
*en **hoom**-mer*
a Lobster

HVITTING
***vit**-ting*
Whiting

KOLJE
***kool**yer*
Haddock

en KRABBE
*en **crab**-ber*
a Crab

KREPS
kreps
Crayfish

LAKS
lax
Salmon

LUTEFISK
***loot**er fisk*
dried Cod in
potash lye

MAKRELL
*mak-**rell***
Mackerel

REKER
***rayk**er*
Shrimps

RØDSPETTE
***rur spet**-ter*
Plaice

SARDINER
*sar**deen**er*
Sardines

SEI
say
Coley

SILD
sil
Herring

SJØTUNGE
***shur toong**-er*
Dover Sole

TORSK/-erogn
torshk/-er rohn
Cod/-Roe

TUNFISK
***toon** fisk*
Tuna

ØRRET
ur-ret
Trout

ÅL
awl
Eel

(in *English* order)

En kilo ...
En sheelo ...
A kilo of ... please.

★

asparges/grønne BØNNER
grurner burner
green Beans

RØDBETER
rur bayter
Beetroot

HODEKAL
hooder kawl
Cabbage

RØDKÅL
rur kawl
red Cabbage

GULRØTTER
gool rurter
Carrots

et BLOMKÅLHODE
ett bloomkawl hooder
a Cauliflower

MAIS
maa-eess
Corn

en AGURK
en ag-goork
a Cucumber

PURRELØK
purra lurk
Leeks

et SALATHODE
ett sa-laat hooder
a Lettuce

SJAMPINJONGER/SOPP
shampeen-yonger/sop
Mushrooms

LØK
lurk
Onions

ERTER
airter
Peas

SPINAT
spi-naat
Spinach

ROSENKÅL
roossen kawl
Sprouts

Jeg vil ha
Yay vil haa
I'd like (some)

en POSE
en poosser
a Bag

en grønn/rød/gul PAPRIKA
grurn/rur/gool pappry-ka
a green/red/yellow Pepper

POTETER
po-tayter
Potatoes

SURKÅL
soor kawl
Sauerkraut

KÅLRABI
kawl raaby
Swedes

TOMATER
to-maater
Tomatoes

Fruit – Frukt *(frookt)*

EPLER
epler
Apples

APRIKOSER
appry-koosser
Apricots

MORELLER
mor-reller
tart red Cherries

KIRSEBÆR
kisher bair
black Cherries

DRUER
droo-er
Grapes

en SITRON
en si-troon
a Lemon

en MELON
en meloon
a Melon

APPELSINER
apple-seener
Oranges

en FERSKEN
en fairsh-ken
a Peach

PÆRER
pearer
Pears

en ANANAS
en anna-nass
a Pineapple

PLOMMER
plom-mer
Plums

SVISKER
svisker
Prunes

BRINGEBÆR
bring-er bair
Raspberries

Frukt og grønnsaker

BANANER
banaaner
Bananas

BLÅBÆR
blaw bair
Bil/Blueberries

BJØRNEBÆR
b-yurner bair
Blackberries

SOLBÆR
sool bair
Blackcurrants

MULTER
moolter
Cloudberries

TYTTEBÆR
tit-ter bair
Cranberries

STIKKELSBÆR
stick-elss bair
Gooseberries

en GRAPEFRUKT
en grape frookt
a Grapefruit

RIPS
rips
Redcurrants

RABARBRA
rab-barbrer
Rhubarb

NYPER
neeper
Rosehips

JORDBÆR
yoor bair
Strawberries

★ Jeg vil ha ...
Yay vil haa ...
I'd like some ...

ØL
url
Beer

OLJE
***ool**-yer*
Oil

KJEKS
sheks
Biscuits/Cookies

PÅLEGG
***paw**leg*
Sandwich fillings

SMØR
smur
Butter

VASKEPULVER
***vask**er **pool**ver*
Soap powder

OST (Geitost)
*oost (**yayt**oost)*
Cheese (Goat's cheese)

SUKKER
***sook**-ker*
Sugar

KAFFE (pulverkaffe)
***kaf**-fer*
Coffee (instant coffee)

TE/TEPOSER
*tay/**tay** poosser*
Tea/Tea bags

EGG
egg
Eggs

TOALETTPAPIR
*twa-**let** pappeer*
Toilet paper

FRUKTSAFT
frookt saft
Fruit juice

OPPVASKMIDDEL
***op**vask middle*
Washing-up liquid

HONNING
***hon**-ning*
Honey

MINERALVANN
*minna-**raal** van*
bottled Water

SYLTETØY
***silt**er-tay*
Jam

YOGHURT
***yoh**-goort*
Yogurt

MARGARIN
*margha-**reen***
Margarine

SALT/PEPPER
*sal-t/**pep**-per*
Salt/Pepper

hel/lett/skummet MELK (MJØLK)
*hayl/let/**skum**-met melk*
whole/semi-/skimmed Milk

SENNEP/KETCHUP
***sen**-nep/**ket**chup*
Mustard/Ketchup

Klær – *klair* – Clothes

en (ski)Lue
en (shee) loo-er
a woolly Hat

en Skjorte/Bluse
en shorter/bloosser
a Shirt/Blouse

en Badedrakt
en baader drakt
Swimming Costume/Trunks

Truser
troosser
Underpants/Briefs

en Kjole
en shooler
a Dress *(en dress* – a suit)

et par Shorts
ett par shorts
a pair of Shorts

en Bukse/Nikkers
en bookser/nikkersh
Trousers/Breeches

et Skjørt
ett shurt
a Skirt

Strømpebukser
strumper bookser
Tights

en Jakke
en yak-ker
a Jacket

en Genser
en ghenser
a Sweater

Sokker
sok-ker
Socks

et Belte
ett belter
a Belt

en Regnfrakk
en rain frak
a Raincoat

et Skjerf
ett shairf
a Scarf

Sko/Støvler
skoo/sturvler
Shoes/Boots

et Lommetørkle
ett lum-mer turkler
a Handkerchief

Hansker/Votter
hansker/vot-ter
Gloves/Mittens

1. **Treng**-er doo **yelp**?
   Hello, can I help you?
3. **Vilk**en **stur**elser?
   What size do you take?
2. Yay skal haa en **ghen**ser.
   I'd like a sweater.
4. Yay **broo**-ker furty. **Kan**doo ta mawl?
   I take size 40. Can you measure me?
5. Har doo **den**-ner ee **blot**?
   Have you got this in blue?

1. **Faw**yay **prur**ver den?
   Can I try it on?
3. Den air for **stoor/leet**'n.
   It's too big/small.
5. Den air **bil**-ly/dear.
   It's cheap/dear.
2. Den **pas**-ser **oot**-mairket.
   It fits very well.
4. Den **pas**-ser **ik**-ker.
   It doesn't fit.

Methods of payment

1. Jeg tar denne. Hvor mye blir det?
2. Betal ved kassa.
3. Tar dere kredittkort/Eurosjekker/reisesjekker, engelske/amerikanske penger?
4. Vær så god.
5. Mange takk.

KASSE

1. *Yay tar **den**-ner. Vor **mee**-er bleer day?*
   I'll take this one. How much is it?

3. *Tar **day**rer kre-**deet** kort/ **uro-/rayser shek**ker, **eng**-elsker/ amry-**kansk**er **peng**-er?*
   Do you take credit cards/ Eurocheques/traveller's cheques, English/American currency?

2. *Be**taal** vay **kas**-ser.*
   Please pay at the cash desk.

4. *Vair saw **goo**.*
   Here you are.

5. ***Mang**-er tak.*
   Thank you.

Apoteket – *appoo-tayker* – the Chemist/Drugstore

Medicines are only sold at an *Apotek*, and the range available without a prescription is limited. The *Parfymeri* and *Supermarked* sell toiletries (p.36).

Vakttjeneste søn- og helligdager kl. 17-20
Duty chemist Sundays & holidays 5-8pm

Åpen dag og natt, søn- og helligdager
Open day & night, Suns. & holidays

Har du noe som hjelper for – ?
*Har doo **noo**-er som **yelp**er for —?*
Have you anything for — ?

Nattåpent
Open at night

Forkjølelse	Diaré	Hodepine	vondt i Magen
*for-**shurl**elser*	*dee-a **ray***	***hoo**der **peen**er*	*voont ee **maag**-en*
a Cold	Diarrhoea	a Headache	Stomach Ache
Forstoppelse	vondt i Øret	Insektstikk	Solbrenthet
*for-**stopp**elser*	*voont ee **ur**-a*	*in**sekt** stick*	***sool**brent hate*
Constipation	Earache	an Insect Bite	Sunburn
Hoste	Høyfeber	vondt i Halsen	Kvalme
***hoos**ter*	*hay **fay**ber*	*voont ee **halsen***	*k-**valm**er*
a Cough	Hay Fever	a Sore Throat	Travel Sickness

(*See also* Medical section p.65, Parts of the body p.68.)

Jeg vil ha —
Yay vil haa —
I'd like —

SÅRSALVE
***sore salv**er*
Antiseptic Cream

SJAMPO
***sham**-poo*
Shampoo

SMERTESTILLENDE
TABLETTER
***smairt**er-**stiller**na
ta**blet**-ter*
some Aspirin

noe VATT
***noo**-er vat*
some Cottonwool

DAMEBIND (TAMPONGER)
***daam**er-bin (tam-**pong**er)*
Sanitary Napkins/Towels (Tampons)

KONDOMER
*kon-**dohm**er*
Condoms

LOMMETØRKLEPAPIR
lum**ma-turkla pa**ppeer
Paper Handkerchiefs

en BANDASJE
*en ban-**daash**er*
a Bandage

SÅRPLASTER
***sore plast**er*
Plasters/Band-Aid

et BARBERBLA
*ett bar-**bair** blaa*
a Razor

BARNEMAT/BARNESALVE
***barn**er maat/**salv**er*
some Baby Food/Cream

INSEKTMIDDEL
***in**sect middle*
Insect Repellant

SÅPE
***sawp**er*
some Soap

BLEIER
***blay**er*
Nappies/Diapers

SOLBRILLER
***sool bril**-ler*
some Sunglasses

TANNPASTA
***tan** pasta*
Toothpaste

en DEODORANT
*en **dayodor-ant***
a Deodorant

en TANNBØRSTE
*en **tan burst**er*
a Toothbrush

en KAM
en kam
a Comb

SOLKREM/OLJE
***sool** kraym/**ool**-yer*
Suntan Cream/Oil

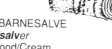

Kiosk *(shosk):* small, everyday items – bus/tram tickets, postcards, newspapers, films, sweets & ice cream, cigarettes. **Bokhandel** *(book handle):* books, stationery, cards, maps. Or try the **Supermarked** or **Stormagasin** (department store).

en (norsk-engelsk) ORDBOK
*en (norshk/**eng**-elsk) **oor**-book*
a (Norwegian-English)
 Dictionary

en BOK
en book
a Book

et KART
ett kart
a Map

en (engelsk) AVIS
*en (**eng**-elsk) av-**veess***
an (English) Newspaper

en FILM (til dias)
*en film (til **dee**-ass)*
a Film (for slides)

en PENN
en pen
a Pen

et FRIMERKE
*ett **free**-mairker*
a Stamp

et POSTKORT
*ett **posst** kort*
a Postcard

en BLYANT
*en blee-**ant***
a Pencil

en BOKSÅPNER
*en **box awp**ner*
a Tin/Can Opener

TOBAKK

en GASSFLASKE
*en **gas flask**er*
a Camping Gaz Bottle

FYRSTIKKER
***feer stik**-ker*
Matches

en LOMMELYKT
*en **lum**-mer likt*
a Torch/Flashlight

en LIGHTER
*en **light**er*
a Lighter

et BATTERI
*ett batter-**ree***
a Battery

SYTRÅD
***see** trawd*
Thread

(filter) SIGARETTER
*(**filter**) sigaret-ter*
(filter) Cigarettes

en KORKETREKKER
*en **corker trek**-ker*
a Corkscrew

en NÅL
en nawl
a Needle

en SAKS
en sax
some Scissors

en FLASKEÅPNER
*en **flasker awp**ner*
a Bottle Opener

et KJØLEELEMENT
*ett **shurler** eller-**ment***
an Ice Pack

HYSSING, SNOR, TAU
***his**-sing, snoor, t-ow*
String, Cord, Rope

Banking hours are 8am–3.30pm Monday to Friday. Minibanks (cash dispensers) take most international credit cards.

You can change money at all banks, Post Offices, airports and major railway stations.

Public holidays – *Offentlige helligdager*
(All shops, banks, etc. close early on Christmas Eve and the Saturday before Easter.)

New Year's Day	January 1	*Nyttårsdag*
Maundy Thursday	March/April	*Skjærtorsdag*
Good Friday	"	*Langfredag*
Easter Monday	"	*Annen påskedag*
May Day	May 1	*Første mai*
Independence Day	May 17	*Grunnlovsdagen*
Ascension Day	May	*Kristi himmelfartsdag*
Whit Monday	May/June	*Annen pinsedag*
Christmas Day	December 25	*Første juledag*
Boxing Day	December 26	*Annen juledag*

1. *Vor* **kanyay** **vex**ler **peng**-er?
   Where can I change money, please?

2. **Oon**-shull, vor **fin**-ner yay **nair**mester bank?
   Excuse me, where is the nearest bank?

3. *Dair* **borter**, paw **torg**-er.
   Over there, in the marketplace.

bankkort	kontanter	en mynt/seddel	penger	valuta
bank kort	*kon-tanter*	*en mint/sed-dle*	*peng-er*	*valooter*
banker's card	cash	a coin/note	money	foreign currency

1. **Fawyay** **vex**ler **noo**-en **eng**-elsker poon/ **doll**ar/ **uro shek**-ker/ **ray**ser **shek**-ker?
   Can I change some pounds/ dollars/ Eurocheques/ traveller's cheques?

2. **Pas**-ser, tak.
   Your passport, please.

3. **Oona**-skreev **hair**.
   Please sign here.

Unnskyld, hvor er Postkontoret?
Oon-shull, vor air **posst** kon-**tor**er?

Where is the post office, please?

Buying stamps – *Frimerker*

1. Kan jeg få et frimerke til dette brevet (postkort)?

2. Til Storbritannia/U.S.A.

3. Hvor mye?

Kiosks also sell stamps.
pakke post – parcels
med luftpost –
by airmail

The Post Office changes money too:
(Reise) valuta –
foreign currency

1. **Kan**yay faw ett **free**-mairker til **det**-ter **bray**ver **(posst** kort)?
   Could I have a stamp for this letter (postcard), please?

2. Til **Stoor** Bri-**tan**yer/ Oo Ess Aa.
   To Great Britain/U.S.A.

3. Vor **mee**-er?
   How much is it?

Hvor finner jeg
nærmeste
telefon?

✱

*Vor **fin**-ner yay **nair**mester
teller-**foon**?*
Where is the nearest phone?

Får jeg bruke
telefonen?

✱

***Faw**yay **broo**-ker teller-
foonen?*
Could I use your phone,
please?

Emergency:
See front of telephone directory under *SOS
øyeblikkelig hjelp.* Fire Brigade 001, Police
002, Ambulance 003. Doctor: see yellow
pages under *Leger, Legevakt.*

Directory enquiries: 0180 (within Scandinavia)
0181 (elsewhere)
Operator & English-speaking operator: 0115
Reverse-charge/collect calls: 0115.

Information in English: see directory under
'How to telephone in Norway'.

Ringing home:
Dial 095 then your country code, followed by
your town's code (omit the first 0).
Britain .... dial 095 then   44
U.S. & Canada...... dial 095 then   1
Australia............... dial 095 then   61
New Zealand .... dial 095 then   64
Eire .... dial 095 then 353
(cheap rates 17.00-08.00)

Linje — , takk
***leen**yer — , tak*
Extension — ,
please.

Opptatt
***op**tat*
Engaged

1. *Yay **treng**-er **det**-ter **noom**rer:*
   I'd like this number:

2. ***Kan**yay faw **snak**-ker may – ?*
   Can I speak to — please?

3. *Vem **taal**er yay may?*
   Who's speaking?

4. ***Ik**-ker leg **paw**!*
   Please hold on!

FJORDEN	BREEN	ØYA	VATNET	FJELLET
f-**yoor**en	**bray**-en	ay-a	**van**-ner	f-**yell**er
the Fjord	the Glacier	the Island	the Lake	the Mountain

Byen – *bee-en* – **The Town**

BANKEN	SLOTTET	HOTELLET	MUSEET
banken	**slot**-ter	hoo-**teller**	moo-**sayer**
the Bank	the Castle, Palace	the Hotel	the Museum
BROEN	KIRKEN	TORGET	PARKEN
broo-en	**sheerk**en	**torg**-er	**parrk**en
the Bridge	the Church	the Marketplace	the Park

ELVEN	DALEN	FOSSEN	SKOGEN
elven	**daal**en	**fos**-sen	**skoog**-en
the River	the Valley	the Waterfall	the Wood, Forest

NORD
noor
North

ØST
urst
East

VEST
vest •
West

SØR/SYD
sur/seed
South

Hvordan kommer jeg til — ?   Hvor ligger — ?
Vordan **kom**-mer yay til —?   *Vor* **ligg**-er — ?
How do I get to — ?   Where is — ?

OLITIET
*olly-**tee**-a*
olice

UTIKKENE
*oo-**tikk**er-na*
e Shops

SPORTSSTADION
sports staadyoon
the Sports stadium

STASJONEN
*stash-**oon**en*
the Station

TURISTINFORMASJONEN
*too-**rist** informash-**oon**en*
the Tourist Office

Hvor er — ?
Vor air — ?
Where is — ?

1. *Unnskyld, hvor er Parkveien?*

2. *Rett fram og først til høyre.*

3. *Kunne du vise meg på kartet?*

4. *Er det langt?*

1. **Oon**-shull, vor air **Park vay**en?
   Excuse me, where is Park Street?

2. **Ret** fram oh **furst** til **hay**rer.
   Straight ahead and then first right.

3. **Koon**-ner doo **veess**er may paw **kart**er?
   Could you show me on the map please?

4. *Air day **langt**?*
   Is it far?

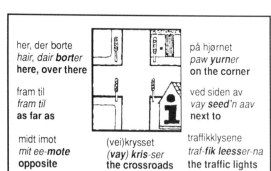

her, der borte *hair, dair **borter*** **here, over there**	på hjørnet *paw yurner* **on the corner**
fram til *fram til* **as far as**	ved siden av *vay **seed**'n aav* **next to**
midt imot *mit ee-**mote*** **opposite**	(vei)krysset *(**vay**) **kris**-ser* **the crossroads**	traffikklysene *traf-**fik leess**er-na* **the traffic lights**

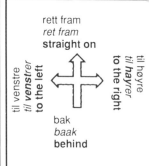

rett fram
ret fram
straight on

til venstre
*til **venstr**er*
to the left

til høyre
*til **hay**rer*
to the right

bak
baak
behind

Toalettet/W.C.
*twa-**lett**er*
The Lavatory

W.C.

Ledig
Vacant

Herrer/Menn
Gents.

Damer/Kvinner
Ladies

Opptatt
Engaged

bussen
boos-sen
the bus

motorsykkelen
mootor **sikk**er-len
the motorcycle

bilen
beelen
the car

en drosjeholdeplass
droh-sher **holl**er plass
a taxi stand

en taxi/drosje
en taxi/**droh**-sher
a taxi

sykkelen
sikker-len
the bicycle

God Tur!
goo toor!
Have a good trip!

jeg går
yay gaw
I walk

stien
stee-en
the path

Mountain passes are often closed late autumn – mid-May. Mountainous terrain and ferries combined can make it difficult to cover more than 100 miles in a day, particularly in the west. Dipped headlights are compulsory at all times.
Speed limits: 30km/19mph, 50km/31mph, 80km/50mph.

In Town

sentrum
Town Centre

Gjelder ikke
buss og taxi

Does not apply to
buses and taxis

Compulsory right turn

*Avgift – fee.
See also p.47

**Ingen
Adgang**
No entry

stengt
closed

Bomveg	**Abonnement**	**Mynt/Coin**	**Manuell**
*Toll road	Season tickets	Automatic	Change given

To park (or not ...) en Parkeringsplass *(parkairingss plass)* a car park

Avgift	1 time	**Maks. P-tid**
Fee	1 hour	Max. parking time

P-Automat
Ticket machine

Maks. 3 timer mot avgift	Instructions:
	Legg i en mynt om gangen.
	Vri mot høyre til stopp.
Max. 3 hours	Insert one coin at a time.
fee payable	Turn to right until stops.
	Annullering
	Cancel

08-17
(09-15)
8-5 Mon-Fri
(9-3 Sat)

P hus   **P** ledig   **P** Langtid **FULLT**   **Kundeparkering**

Multi-storey   Spaces   Long-term parking full   Customer parking

Parkering forbudt/forbode

No parking

No parking zone

Residents only. Park ONLY at meters.

Datoparkering: night parking one side of street only (even numbers on even days, odd numbers on odd days)

Motorvei – Motorway/Expressway **Utkjørsel** – Exit **Stengt** – Closed

Your right of way

Right of way cancelled

Farlig veikryss
Dangerous crossroads

Motor vehicles only

Falling stones

Animals crossing

M

Passing place

Ferist – cattle grid

| Bom(veg) |
| Toll (road) |
| **Stop** |
| **Avgift** |
| **06-22** |

Stop:Toll
6am–10pm

Bratte bakker
Steep hills

| Høyfjellsveger |
| nattestengt |
| stengt alle dager |
| normalt åpent hele |
| døgnet |

Mountain roads
closed at night
always closed
usually open 24 hours

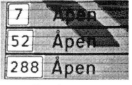

Roads open

Nødtelefon
Emergency phone

| Grusvei | Kjør sakte | Svake kanter |

Gravelled road   Drive slowly   Soft verges

(see pp.41, 49, 65)

Bensin		Totaktsblanding	
*ben**seen***		***too** takts **blan**-ning*	
Petrol/Gas		2-stroke mix	
Super		Luft	
***soop**er*		*looft*	
Super		Air	
Blyfri		Olje	
***blee** free*		***ool**-yer*	
Unleaded		Oil	
Diesel		Vann	
***dees**sel*		*van*	
Diesel		Water	

*Vor air **nair**mester ben**seen** stash-**oon**?*
Where is the nearest filling station?

All are self-service and take credit cards. In isolated areas fill up at every opportunity.

Åpent hele døgnet / 24 timer – open 24 hours
Seddelautomat – petrol dispenser: takes notes.

1. *Shekk **ool**-yen (**looft trik**-ker).*
   Please check the oil (tyre pressure).

2. *Vor **mee**-er bleer day?*
   How much is that?

Breakdowns and Repairs

1. Jeg har fått motorstopp. Kan du hjelpe meg?
2. Får jeg bruke telefonen?
3. Hvor er nærmeste verksted?
4. Hvor står bilen nå?

1. *Yay har fot **moot**or stop. **Kan**doo **yelp**er may?*
   I have broken down. Can you help me, please?

2. ***Faw**yay **broo**-ker teller-**foon**en?*
   Can I use your phone, please?

3. *Vor air **nair**mester **vairk**stayd?*
   Where is the nearest garage?

4. *Vor stor **beelen naw**?*
   Where is the car now?

Emergency telephones and help: pp. 47 and 65.

Mek. Verksted – Repairs

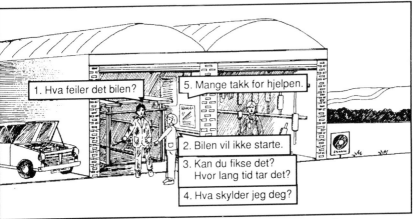

1. Hva feiler det bilen?
5. Mange takk for hjelpen.
2. Bilen vil ikke starte.
3. Kan du fikse det? Hvor lang tid tar det?
4. Hva skylder jeg deg?

1. *Va **fayl**er day **beel**en?*
   What's the matter with the car?

2. ***Beel**en vil **ik**-ker **start**er.*
   My car won't start.

3. ***Kan**doo **fix**er day? Vor lang **tee** tar day?*
   Can you repair it? How long will it take?

4. *Va **shul**-ler yay **day**?*
   What do I owe you?

5. ***Mang**-er tak for **yelp**en.*
   Many thanks for your help.

On Two and Four Wheels

Jeg trenger en —
*Yay **treng**-er en —*
I need a —

Jeg får motorstopp.
*Yay faw **moot**or stop.*
The engine is stalling.

— virker ikke.
*— **veer**ker **ik**-ker.*
The — isn't working.

Motoren er gått varm (fusker).
***Moot**oren air got **varm** (**foos**ker).*
The engine is overheating (misfiring).

Car, Bicycle and Motorcycle parts (in *English* order)

1. LUFTFILTERET
   looft filter-a
   the Air Filter

2. BATTERIET
   batter-reeyer
   the Battery

3. BREMSENE
   bremsser-na
   the Brakes

4. BREMSEKLOSSENE
   bremsser klosser-na
   the Brake Blocks

5. en LYSPÆRE
   en leess pairer
   a Bulb

6. KJETTINGEN
   shetting-en
   the Cable

7. FORGASSEREN
   for-gasser-en
   the Carburettor

8. KJEDEN
   shayden
   the Chain

9. CHOKEN
   shawken
   the Choke

10. KLUTSJEN
    clutchen
    the Clutch

11. FORDELEREN
    for-dayleren
    the Distributor

12. det ELEKTRISKE SYSTEMET
    day aylektrisker sistaymer
    the Electrics

13. MOTOREN
    mootor-en
    the Engine

14. EKSOSEN
    ek-soossen
    the Exhaust

15. VIFTEREMMEN
    vifter rem-men
    the Fan Belt

16. FREMGAFFELEN
    frem gaffel-en
    the Front Fork

17. en SIKRING
    en sikring
    a Fuse

18. en PAKNING
    en packning
    a Gasket

19. GIRET
    gearer
    the Gear

20. STYRET
    steerer
    the Handlebars

1. en SYKKELSLANGE
en sik-kel slang-er
an Inner Tube

2. NØKKELEN
nurklen
the Key

3. en Olje/Vann LEKKASJE
ool-yer/van lekkaasher
an Oil/Water Leak

4. LYKTEN
likten
the Light

5. BAGASJEBRETTET
ba-gaasher bret-ter
the Luggage Carrier

6. en BAGASJEREM
en ba-gaasher raym
a Luggage Strap

7. en SKVETTSKJERM
en sk-vet shairm
a Mudguard

8. en MUTTER
en moot-ter
a Nut

9. en BENSINKANNE
en ben-seen can-ner
a Petrol Can

10. STIFTENE
stifter-na
the Points

11. et SYKKEL-
REPARASJONSUTSTYR
repparash-oons ootsteer
a Cycle Puncture Kit

12. PUMPEN
pumpen
the Pump

13. RADIATOREN
raad-yaatoren
the Radiator

14. en SALTASKE
en saal tasker
a Saddlebag

15. en SKRUE, BOLT
en screw-er, bolt
a Screw, Bolt

16. en SKRUTREKKER
en screw trek-ker
a Screwdriver

37. en STØTDEMPER
en sturt demper
a Shock Absorber

38. LYDPOTTEN
leed pot'n
the Silencer

39. en SKIFTENØKKEL
en shifter nurkel
a Spanner

40. en TENNPLUGG
en ten plug
a Sparking Plug

41. EIKENE
ayker-na
the Spokes

42. et DEKK
ett deck
a Tyre

43. LUFTTRYKKET
looft trik-ker
the Tyre Pressure

44. en VENTIL
en ven-teel
a Valve

45. et HJUL
ett yool
a Wheel

46. FRONTRUTA
fron-t roota
the Windscreen/shield

47. VINDUSVISKERNE
vindooss visker-na
the Wipers

KJETTINGER, PIGGDEKK
shetting-er, pig deck
Snow Chains, Studded Tyres

Jeg har punktert
Yay har poonk-tairt
I've got a Puncture/Flat

en (STYRT)HJELM
en (steert) yelm
a Crash Helmet

Sykkelutleie

Bicycle hire

1. *Goo**daag**. Yay **skul**-ler **yairn**er **layer** en **beel**.*
   Hello, I'd like to hire a car.

2. *Va slaags beel – leet'n, stoor?*
   What sort of car – small, large?

1. *Vor **leng**-er? En daag, en **ook**er?*
   How long for? For a day, a week?

2. *Va air **preess**en pair **dayn**/dep**poss**itum?*
   What is the rate per day/the deposit?

3. ***Kan**yay lev**vair**er den **in** e **Tron**yem?*
   Can I leave the car in Trondheim?

4. *Hair air mit **sairtiffy**-kaat.*
   Here is my driving licence.

en billett/billetter
– ticket/s

2. Én vei eller tur-retur?

1. En (to) til Bergen, takk.

3. Én vei. Hvor mye blir det?

4. Jeg vil gjerne bestille plass (ligge-/soveplass).

Hvor skal du?	tur-retur
*Vor **skal** doo?*	**toor** rettoor
Where are you going?	return/round trip
Jeg skal til —	Røyker/ikke-
Yay skal til —	røyker
I'm going to —	**rayker/ik**-ker
	rayker
én vei	
ain vay	Smoker/Non-
single/one way	smoker

. Ain (too) til **Bairg**-en, tak.
   One (two) to Bergen, please.

. Ain vay **el**-ler **toor** rettoor?
   Single or return (round trip)?

. Ain vay. Vor **mee**-e bleer day?
   Single. How much is it?

4. Yay vil **yair**ner bestiller **plass** (**ligg**er-/**sov**er-plass).
   Can I book a seat (couchette/ sleeper)?

‌Husk å bestille plassbillett – ellers står du der. Remember to book a seat – or ‌ou'll have to stand.

. Vor gaw **Yurt**er-bory **tawg**-er fra?
   Where does the Gothenburg train go from?

‌. Fra **platt**form (spoor) **feer**er.
   From platform four.

. Norr gaw *****tawg**-er?
   When does the *train go?

‌neste/siste tog
‌**ester/sist**er tawg
‌ext/last train

‌ypes of ticket, Finding a seat ‌nd Local travel p.56.

1. Hvor går Göteborg- toget fra?

2. Fra plattform (spor) fire.

3. Når går *toget?

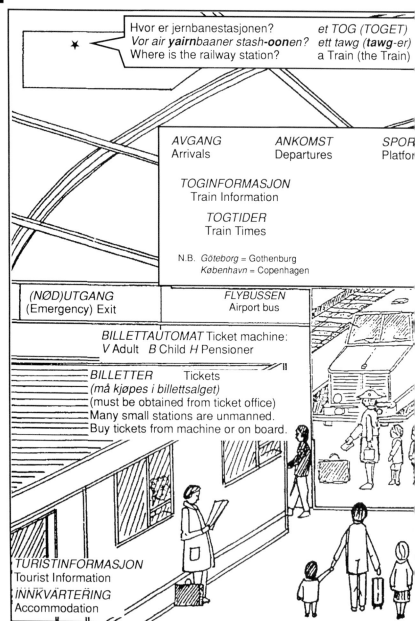

Hvor er jernbanestasjonen?
Vor air **yairn**baaner stash-**oon**en?
Where is the railway station?

et TOG (TOGET)
ett tawg (**tawg**-er)
a Train (the Train)

AVGANG — Arrivals

ANKOMST — Departures

SPOR — Platfor

TOGINFORMASJON — Train Information

TOGTIDER — Train Times

N.B. *Göteborg* = Gothenburg
København = Copenhagen

(NØD)UTGANG — (Emergency) Exit

FLYBUSSEN — Airport bus

BILLETTAUTOMAT Ticket machine:
V Adult   B Child   H Pensioner

BILLETTER   Tickets
(må kjøpes i billettsalget)
(must be obtained from ticket office)
Many small stations are unmanned.
Buy tickets from machine or on board.

TURISTINFORMASJON — Tourist Information

INNKVARTERING — Accommodation

en *RUTETABELL* – Timetable
fra: from *til:* to *natt til søndag:* **Sat.** night
alle dager/netter: daily/nightly *bare:* only

hverdager/Hvd: weekdays (Mon-Fri
unntatt lørdag/u lø: except Saturday
søn- & helligdager/Hld: Sun. & holi

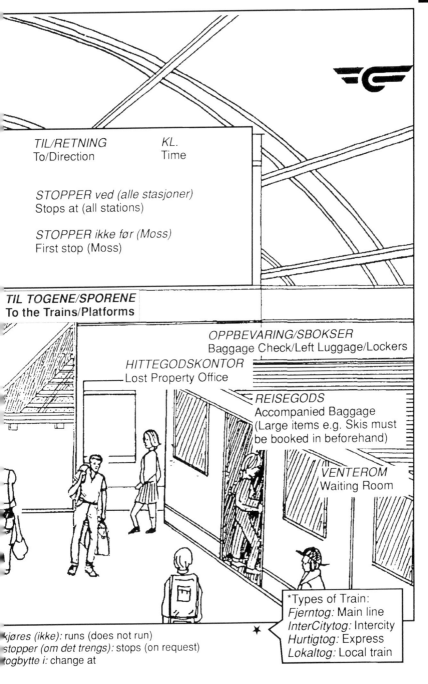

TIL/RETNING   *KL.*
To/Direction   Time

STOPPER ved (alle stasjoner)
Stops at (all stations)

STOPPER ikke før (Moss)
First stop (Moss)

TIL TOGENE/SPORENE
To the Trains/Platforms

OPPBEVARING/SBOKSER
Baggage Check/Left Luggage/Lockers

HITTEGODSKONTOR
Lost Property Office

REISEGODS
Accompanied Baggage
(Large items e.g. Skis must
be booked in beforehand)

VENTEROM
Waiting Room

*Types of Train:
Fjerntog: Main line
InterCitytog: Intercity
Hurtigtog: Express
Lokaltog: Local train

kjøres (ikke): runs (does not run)
stopper (om det trengs): stops (on request)
togbytte i: change at

RØYKING FORBUDT
No smoking

*Use this to ask for a seat anywhere – bus, park bench, café, etc.

*1. *Air **den**-ner **plas**-sen **lay**dy?*
   Is this seat free?

2. *Yay troor **den**-ner **plas**-sen ai meen.*
   I think that's my seat.

3. *Air **det**-ter **tawg**-er til **Liller**-hammer?*
   Is this the train for Lillehammer?

Local transport T-banen *tay baanen* Underground/Subway

Tickets: All tickets are flat fare and are valid on trams, buses and the T-banen. *Enkeltbillett –* single ticket., *Dagskort –* 24 hour ticket, *7 dagers kort –* 7 day ticket: both can be used by several people, but only one at a time. *Flexikort –* ten detachable tickets, each allowing one change within the hour: stamp it in the machine when you get on first. (Buy season tickets beforehand at ticket offices, Tourist Information, kiosks, post offices.) *Billettsalg hos fører –* tickets from driver.

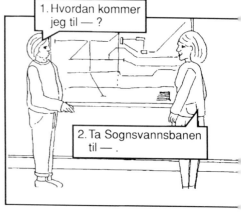

1. *Vordan **kom**-mer yay til — ?*
   How do I get to — ?

2. *Taa **Sogg'ns**vanss **baanen** til — .*
   Take the Sognsvann line to — .

ingen avstigning
do not alight

stopper på signal
request stop

stoppested
bus/tram/T-bane stop

en trikk/trikken
a tram/the tram

utgang bak
exit at rear

1. *Norr gaw* **boos**-*sen til* **Awn**dalss ness?*
   What time is the bus for Åndalsnes?

| *en buss/bussen* | a bus/the bus |

2. *Vor* **stop**-per **boos**-sen til **Yur**-veek?*
   Where does the bus for Gjøvik stop?

| *bussterminalen}* *rutebilstasjonen }* | the bus station |

3. **Maw**yay **bit**-ter **booss**?*
   Do I have to change buses?

1. *Gaw* **den**-ner (**boos**-sen) til **Yay**loo?*
   Does this (bus) go to Geilo?

2. *Air* **det**-ter stash-**oon**en?*
   Is this the station?

bryggen, kaien	havnen	Båttur
brigg-en, k-**eye**-en	**haav**nen	bawt toor
the Quay	the Harbour	Boat trip

Båtutleie
bawt oot-layer
Boats for hire

← TIL KAIEN

1. Når går Bodø-båten?
2. Hvor fra?
3. Hvor lang tid tar det?
4. Kan jeg reservere en lugar/køye?

*1.Kan jeg få leie en båt?
Kanyay faw **layer** en **bawt**?
Can I hire a boat?

en ferge/fergen
en **fair**yer/**fair**yen
a Ferry/the ferry

(LIVS)FARE!
faarer
DANGER

Babord	Styrbord
baaboor	**steerboo**
Port	Starboard

1. *Norr gaw* **Bood**ur *bawt'n?*
   When does the boat to Bodø go?
2. *Vor fra?*
   Where from?
3. *Vor lang* **tee** *tar day?*
   How long does it take?
4. **Kan**yay *ressair*-**vairer** *en loo*-**gar/kay**er?
   Can I book a cabin/bunk?

et livbelte
ett **leev belt**er
a Lifebelt

livbåten
leev bawt'n
the Lifeboat

Gjestehavn
yester haav'n
Visitors' harbour

stranden
strann'n
the Beach

sjøen, vatnet
shuh-en, **van**-ner
the Sea/Lake

øya
ay-er
the Island

en motorbåt
en **moot**or bawt
a Motorboat

en lystbåt, yacht
en **list** bawt, yot
a Yacht

en robåt
en **roo** bawt
a Rowing Boat

en gummibåt
en **gum**-my baw▮
a Rubber Dinghy

tolleren
toller-en
the Customs Officer

registreringshavn
*rayghee-**strair**ingss haav'n*
the Port of Registry

1. Hvor finner jeg en jernvareforretning?

2. Hvor får jeg tak i vann/dieselolje/isblokker?

3. Hvor ligger havnekontoret?

4. Hvor får jeg tak i en skipsmaskinist?

1. *Vor **fin**-ner yay en **yairn**vaarer foret*ning?
   Where is the chandlery?

2. *Vor **faw**yay taak ee van/**deess**el ool-yer/**eess blok**-ker?*
   Where can I get some water/diesel oil/blocks of ice?

3. *Vor **lig**-ger **haav**ner kon-**tor**er?*
   Where is the harbour master's office?

4. *Vor **faw**yay taak ee en **ships** ma**sheen**ist?*
   Where will I find a marine engineer?

★

Hvor får jeg tak i værmeldingen?*
*Vor **faw**yay taak ee **vair mell**ing-en?*
Where can I get a weather forecast?

stormvarsel
*storm **var**sel*
gale warning

høyt/lavtrykk
hayt trik/**laav** trik
high/low pressure

økende/avtakende/moderat vind
urker-na/**aav taaker**-na/**mooder**aat vin
increasing/decreasing/moderate wind

tidevannet, havstrøm
teeder **van**-ner, **haav**-strurm
the tide, current

grovsjø
groov shur
rough sea

vindstille
vin stil-ler
calm

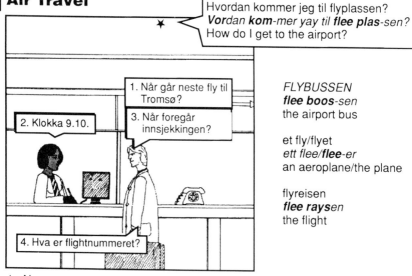

Hvordan kommer jeg til flyplassen?
*Vordan **kom**-mer yay til **flee plas**-sen?*
How do I get to the airport?

1. Når går neste fly til Tromsø?

2. Klokka 9.10.

3. Når foregår innsjekkingen?

4. Hva er flightnummeret?

FLYBUSSEN
flee boos-sen
the airport bus

et fly/flyet
ett flee/flee-er
an aeroplane/the plane

flyreisen
flee raysen
the flight

1. *Norr gaw **nest**er flee til **Troms**ur?*
   When is the next flight to Tromsø?

2. *Klok-ker nee tee.*
   At 9.10.

3. *Norr **fora**-gaw **in**shekking-en?*
   What time is check in?

4. *Va air **flight noom**rer?*
   What is the flight number?

1. Jeg må bytte (bekrefte/avbestille) billetten min.

2. Jeg skal ha en billett til New York på mandag, takk.

1. *Yay maw **bit**-ter (**bekreft**er/**aav** bestiller) bil-**let**'n meen.*
   I'd like to change (confirm/cancel) my reservation.

2. *Yay skal haa en bil-**let** til New York paw **man**daag, tak.*
   I'd like a ticket to New York for Monday, please.

Sightseeing

Hvor er turistkontoret?
Vor air too-rist kon-torer?
Where is the Tourist Office?

1. Hva er severdighetene her?

3. Når er museet åpent?

2. Man kan besøke Folkemuseet, eller gå en tur i skogen.

4. Hver dag fra 10-19 unntatt mandager.

1. *Va air sayvairdy-hayter-na hair?*
   What is there to see here?

3. *Norr air moo-sayer awpent?*
   When is the museum* open?

*Most museums are closed on Mondays.

Gratis adgang	UTSTILLING
Admission Free	Exhibition

2. *Man kan besurker fol-ker moo-sayer, el-ler gaw en toor ee skoog-en.*
   You can visit the folk museum, or go for a walk in the woods.

4. *Vair daag fra tee til nitt'n oontat mandaag-er.*
   *Every day from 10am till 7pm except Mondays.

Theft and lost property

1. Jeg har mistet (passet mitt).

2. (Bag'en min) er blitt stjålet.

3. Hvordan ser den ut?
   Hva hadde du i den?

1. *Yay har mistet (pas-ser mit).*
   I've lost (my passport).

2. *(Beg-en meen) air blit st-yawlet.*
   (My bag) has been stolen.

3. *Vordan sair den oot?*
   Va had-der doo ee den?
   What does it look like?
   What was in it?

kameraet/mitt kamera	pengene/pengene mine	bag'en/bag'en min
cameraa-er/mit camera	*penger-na/penger-na meena*	*beg-en/beg-en meen*
the Camera/my Camera	the Money/my Money	the Bag/my Bag

(Familie)Navn	Adresse	Når?	Hvor?	}?
fa-meelyer naavn	*ah-dresser*	*norr*	*vor*	
(Family) Name	Address	When?	Where?	

1. *Vor gaw day **an** aw **spil**-ler ten-niss/golf – å **gaw** en toor?*
   Where can you play tennis/golf – go for a walk?

2. *Vor kan man **baader/fisker**?*
   Where can you go swimming/fishing?

3. *Treng-er man fisker kort?*
   Do you need a fishing permit?

Et fiskekort: a permit – required for freshwater fishing but not in saltwater.

Winter Sports

1. **Kan**yay faw **noo**-en **shee teem**er?
   Can I have some skiing lessons?

2. *Yaa, day **kan**doo.*
   Yes, of course.

3. **Faw**yay **lay**er **oot**steer? *(alpeen-/langren-/**toor**-shee).*
   Can I hire some equipment? (downhill/cross-country/touring skis)

4. *Yay skal haa ett **hays**er kort (et daags-/**ook**er-kort).*
   I'd like a lift pass (a daily/weekly pass).

Skiing terms

Hoppbakken
hop bak-ken
the Ski Jump

en Kjelke
en **shelk**er
a Sledge

Lysløypa
leess layper
the Floodlit Run

Skibakken
shee bak-ken
the Ski Run

Skiheisen
shee haysen
the Ski Lift

Skiløypa
shee layper
the Ski Run (XC)

Skøyter
shayter
Skates

Taubanen
t-**ow baan**en
the Cable Car

Utfor-, Slalåm-bakke
ootfor-/**slaal**om **bak**-ker
Downhill Run

Utforkjøring
ootfor **shur**-ing
Downhill skiing

On the piste

1. Jeg er nybegynner.

2. Hvor er nybegynnerbakkene?

3. Jeg er flink på ski.

1. *Yay air **nee** beyin-ner.*
    I'm a beginner.

2. *Vor air **nee** beyin-ner **bakk**er-na?*
    Where are the beginners' runs?

3. *Yay air **flink** paw **shee**.*
    I'm good at skiing.

Langrenn
lang ren
Cross-country skiing (XC)

1. *Norr beyin-ner **fora-still**ingen?*
   When does the performance start?

2. ***Faw**yay too bil-**letter** til **lur**daags matti-**nay**en/k-**velss fora-still**ingen?*
   Can I have two tickets for Saturday afternoon/evening?

3. *Vor **mee**-er?*
   What price?

4. ***Seer**ker sexty **kroon**er.*
   About 60 kroner.

1. *Va **air** day som gaw paw sheeno/ tay-**aat**rer ee **daag** (ee morrn k-**vel**)?*
   What's on at the cinema/theatre today (tomorrow evening)?

2. *Yay vil paw **foot**b-al kamp.*
   I'd like to go to a football match.

3. *Har **day**rer **disc**o hair?*
   Is there a disco here?

Accidents and illness

SYKEHUS/SJUKEHUS   *AKUTTEN*
Hospital   Emergencies/Casualty Department

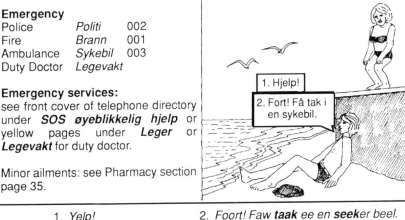

Emergency

Police	*Politi*	002
Fire	*Brann*	001
Ambulance	*Sykebil*	003
Duty Doctor	*Legevakt*	

Emergency services:
see front cover of telephone directory under **SOS øyeblikkelig hjelp** or yellow pages under **Leger** or **Legevakt** for duty doctor.

Minor ailments: see Pharmacy section page 35.

Speech bubbles:
1. Hjelp!
2. Fort! Få tak i en sykebil.

1. *Yelp!*
   Help!

2. *Foort! Faw **taak** ee en **seek**er beel.*
   Quick! Call an ambulance.

Calling the doctor/making an appointment

Speech bubbles:
1. Jeg er syk. Få tak i en lege.
2. Jeg skal til legen. Når passer det å komme?
3. Må jeg bestille time?

en lege/doktor
a doctor

Helsesenter/Legekontor
Health centre/surgery

Kontortid
Consulting hours

eft. avtale
by appointment

1. *Yay air **seek**. Faw **taak** ee en **layg**-er.*
   I'm ill. Please get a doctor.

2. *Yay skal til **layg**-en. Norr **pas**-ser day aw **kom**-mer?*
   I'd like to see the doctor. When can I come?

3. ***Maw**yay be**stil**-ler **teem**er?*
   Do I have to make an appointment?

Under a reciprocal agreement UK citizens are entitled to the same medical care as Norwegians. Ambulances and hospital treatment are free; doctors' fees may be refunded by the *Trygdekasse*. Prescriptions and dental treatment are not refundable.

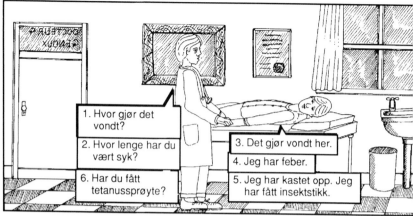

1. *Vor yur day **voont**?*
   Where does it hurt?

2. *Vor **leng**-er har doo vairt **seek**?*
   How long have you been ill?

6. *Har doo fot **tet**anuss **spray**ter?*
   Have you been vaccinated
   against tetanus?

3. *Day yur voont **hair**.*
   It hurts here.

4. *Yay har **fay**ber.*
   I have a temperature.

5. *Yay har **kast**et op. Yay har fot
   insect stick.*
   I've been sick. I've been stung.

I. *Yay **broo**-ker **den**-ner meddy-**seen**
   rayg-el messy.*
   I take this medicine regularly.

2. ***Koon**-ner yay faw en res-**sept**?*
   Could you give me a
   prescription, please?

6. *Va **shul**-ler yay?*
   What do I owe you?

3. *Doo **maw** ik-ker **speess**er ...
   (**drik**-ker)*
   You must not eat ... (drink)

4. *Vor **gam**-mel air han (**hoon**)?*
   How old is he (she)?

5. *Han (**hoon**) air fem.*
   He (she) is five.

When to take your medicine:

før/etter mat
before/after meals

... ganger om dagen
... times a day

hver dag/time
every day/hour

i ... dager
for ... days

om morgenen/kvelden
in the morning/at night

oppløses i vann
dissolve in water

suges
suck

svelges hel
swallow whole

til utvortes/innvortes bruk
for external/internal use

What the doctor needs to know:

Jeg har ... *Yay har ...* I have ...

astma	***astmer***	asthma
diabetes	*dee-abetess*	diabetes
epilepsi	*epilep-see*	epilepsy

dårlig hjerte	høyt blodtrykk
dorly yairter	*hayt **bloo** trik*
heart trouble	high blood pressure

Jeg er ... *Yay air ...* I'm ...

gravid	allergisk mot (penicillin)
grav-eed	*al-lairg-isk moot*
I'm ... pregnant	allergic to (penicillin)

98.6F = 37°C

At the Dentist –

Tannlegen Tannlegevakt:
duty dentist

Kontortid ... Lørdag eft. avtale
Hours ... Sats. by appointment

1. Jeg har tannverk.

2. Kan jeg få time (så snart som mulig)?

3. Gjør det vondt?

4. Det gjør vondt her.

*Yay har **tan**vairk.*
I've got toothache.

Kanyay faw **teem**er (saw **snart** som mooly)?
Can I make an appointment (as soon as possible)?

3. *Yur day **voont**?*
Does that hurt?

4. *Day yur voont **hair**.*
It hurts here.

Det gjør vondt her.
*Day yur voont **hair**.*
It hurts here.

★

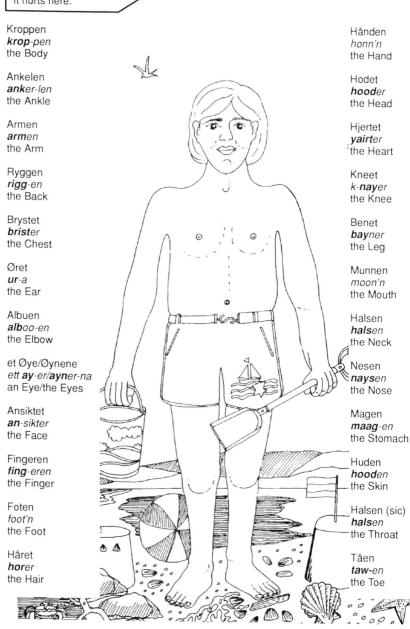

Kroppen
krop-pen
the Body

Ankelen
anker-len
the Ankle

Armen
armen
the Arm

Ryggen
rigg-en
the Back

Brystet
brister
the Chest

Øret
ur-a
the Ear

Albuen
alboo-en
the Elbow

et Øye/Øynene
ett **ay**-er/**ayn**er-na
an Eye/the Eyes

Ansiktet
an-sikter
the Face

Fingeren
fing-eren
the Finger

Foten
foot'n
the Foot

Håret
horer
the Hair

Hånden
honn'n
the Hand

Hodet
hooder
the Head

Hjertet
yairter
the Heart

Kneet
k-**nay**er
the Knee

Benet
bayner
the Leg

Munnen
moon'n
the Mouth

Halsen
halsen
the Neck

Nesen
naysen
the Nose

Magen
maag-en
the Stomach

Huden
hooden
the Skin

Halsen (sic)
halsen
the Throat

Tåen
taw-en
the Toe

1. Morn. Hvordan går det?
2. Bra, takk – og med deg?
3. Jeg heter — . Hva heter du?
4. Dette er min mann/kone, min sønn/datter, min venn/venninne.
5. (Det) gleder meg.
6. Ha det.

1. *Morrn. **Vor**dan **gaw** day?*
   Hallo. How are you?
3. *Yay **hay**ter — . Va **hay**ter **doo**?*
   I'm called —. What's your name?
5. *(Day) **glay**der may.*
   Pleased to meet you.

2. *Braa, tak – oh may **day**?*
   Fine, thanks – and you?
4. ***Det**-ter air meen **man/koon**er, meen surn/**dat**-ter, meen ven/**venin**-ner.*
   This is my husband/wife, my son/daughter, my friend (male/female).
6. ***Hard**er.*
   Goodbye.

1. Dette er min bror (min søster).
2. Har du noen søsken?
3. Hvor gammel er du?
4. Jeg er tretten

1. ***Det**-ter air meen **broor** (meen **surst**er).*
   This is my brother (my sister).
2. *Har doo **noo**-en **susk**en?*
   Have you any brothers and sisters?

3. *Vor **gam**-mel air doo?*
   How old are you?
4. *Yay air **trett**'n.*
   I'm thirteen

1. *Air day **furst**er gang doo air ee*
   ***Norg**-er?*
   Is this your first visit to Norway?
2. ***Treev**ess doo hair?*
   Do you like it here?
4. *Vor **leng**-er har doo **vairt** hair?*
   How long have you been here?
6. *Vor **kom**-mer doo fra?*
   Where do you come from?

3. *Yay **leek**er may veldy **got** hair.*
   I like it very much here.
5. *En **ook**er.*
   For a week.
7. *Yay boor ee **Lonn**-donn.*
   I live in London.

Accepting an invitation

1. *Air doo **op**tat ee k-**vel**?*
   Are you busy this evening?
2. *Har doo **list** til aw **kom**-mer boort til*
   ***oss** (may) ee k-**vel**?*
   Would you like to come and see
   us (me) this evening?

3. *Saw **higg**-erly. Day vil yay **yairn**e.*
   That would be very nice. I'd lov
   to.
4. *Norr (vor) skal vee **murt**ess?*
   When (where) shall we meet?

Visiting

1. Hallo. Hjertelig velkommen! Hyggelig å treffe deg!
2. Hva vil du ha å drikke? (te, kaffe, brus, vin)
3. Vær så god, forsyn deg. Litt til?
4. Ja takk/Nei takk. Jeg er forsynt.
5. Smakte det?
6. Det var deilig!
7. Liker du sport, musikk, dansing, å lese?
8. Jeg er glad i ...

1. *Halloo. **Yairt**erly velkom-men. **Higg**-erly aw **tref**-fer day.*
   Hallo. Welcome! Pleased to meet you!

2. *Va vil doo haa aw **drik**-ker? (tay, **kaf**-fer, brooss, veen)*
   What would you like to drink? (tea, coffee, soft drink, wine)

3. *Vair saw **goo**, for-**sin** day. Lit **til**?*
   Please help yourself. A little more?

4. *Yaa tak/nay tak. Yay air for-**sint**.*
   Yes, please/No thanks, I've had enough.

5. *Smaakter day?*
   Did you like it? (food)

6. *Day var **day**ly!*
   That was delicious!

7. *Leeker doo sport, moo-**sik**, dansing, aw **lays**er?*
   Do you like sport, music, dancing, reading?

8. *Yay air **glaa** ee ...*
   I like ...

Saying goodbye

3. Takk, i like måte.
1. Takk for en deilig kveld. Det var virkelig hyggelig.
2. Takk for nå – og på gjensyn.

1. *Tak for en **day**ly k-**vel**. Day var **virk**erly **higg**-erly.*
   Thank you for a lovely evening. It was really nice.

2. *Tak for **naw** – oh paw **yen**-seen.*
   Goodbye – and see you again.

3. *Tak, ee **leek**er **maw**ter.*
   Thanks, the same to you.

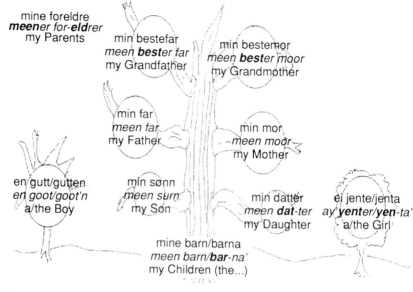

mine foreldre
meener for-**eld**rer
my Parents

min bestefar
meen **best**er far
my Grandfather

min bestemor
meen **best**er moor
my Grandmother

min far
meen far
my Father

min mor
meen moor
my Mother

en gutt/gutten
en goot/**goot**'n
a/the Boy

min sønn
meen surn
my Son

min datter
meen **dat**-ter
my Daughter

ei jente/jenta
ay **yent**er/**yen**-ta'
a/the Girl

mine barn/barna
meen barn/**bar**-na'
my Children (the...)

Countries and Nationalities

Han/hun er norsk.
Han/hoon air norshk.
He/she is Norwegian.

Hvor kommer du fra?
*Vor **kom**-mer doo fra?*
Where do you come from?

Jeg er fra ...
Yay air fra ...
I'm from ...

England	engelsk	Irland	irsk
eng-lan	**eng**-elsk	**eer**lan	**eer**shk
England	English	Ireland	Irish
Skottland	skotsk	Wales	valisisk
skotlan	skotsk	vales	va-**lee**sisk
Scotland	Scottish	Wales	Welsh

Amerika/USA
amerriker/Oo Ess Aa
America/USA

amerikansk
ammry-**kaansk**
American

Australia
ow-**straal**yer
Australia

australsk
ow-**straal**sk
Australian

Canada
kanada
Canada

kanadisk
ka-**naad**isk
Canadian

Ny Zealand
nee **say**lan
New Zealand

nyzealandsk
nee **say**lansk
a New Zealander

om våren	*om **voren***	in spring
	det blåser / *day **blawser*** / it's windy	17. mai / ***sutter**-na **my*** / National Day	
mars / *marsh* / MARCH	Påske / ***pawsk**er* / Easter	april / *app-**reel*** / APRIL	mai / *my* / MAY

om sommeren	*om **sommer**-en*	in summer
	solen skinner / ***soolen shin**-ner* / it's sunny		det er varmt / *day air **varmt*** / it's hot	
juni / *yoony* / JUNE	juli / *yooly* / JULY	jeg er for varm / *yay air for **varm*** / I'm hot	august / *ow-**goost*** / AUGUST

om høsten	*om **hurst**'n*	in autumn/fall
	det regner / *day **rayner*** / it's raining		det er kaldt / *day air **kalt*** / it's cold	
september / *sep**tem**ber* / SEPTEMBER	oktober / *ok**too**ber* / OCTOBER	jeg fryser / *yay **freess**er* / I'm cold	november / *no**vem**ber* / NOVEMBER

om vinteren	*om **vinter**-en*	in winter
	God Jul! / *goo yool* / Merry Christmas!		Godt Nytt År! / *got nit **or*** / Happy New Year!	
desember / *des**sem**ber* / DECEMBER	det snør / *day snur* / it's snowing	januar / *yannoo-**ar*** / JANUARY	februar / *febroo-**ar*** / FEBRUARY

Hva er klokka?
*Va air **klok**-ker?*
What's the time?

N.B. half past = halfway to
Norwegians think of the half hour
as being halfway to the next hour,
e.g half past eight = halv ni.
(If in doubt, use figures,
e.g. åtte tretti = 8.30.)

Klokken er tre
*klok-ken air **tray***
It's <u>three o'clock</u>

fem over tre
***fem awver** tray*
<u>five past</u> three

ti over fire
***tee awver** feerer*
<u>ten past</u> four

kvart over fem
***k-vart awver** fem*
<u>quarter past</u> five

ti på halv sju
***tee paw hal** shoo*
<u>twenty past</u> six

fem på halv åtte
***fem paw hal** ot-ter*
<u>twenty-five past</u> seven

halv ni
***hal** nee*
<u>half past</u> eight

fem over halv ni
***fem awver hal** nee*
<u>twenty-five to</u> nine

ti over halv ti
***tee awver hal** tee*
<u>twenty to</u> ten

kvart på elleve
***k-vart paw** elver*
<u>quarter to</u> eleven

ti på tolv
***tee paw** tol*
<u>ten to</u> twelve

fem på ett
***fem paw** ett*
<u>five to</u> one

(klokka ett – one o'clock)

NB: æ, ø and å are separate letters at the end of the Norwegian alphabet, but are listed here under a and o.

Stop

0	null *nool*	17	sytten *sutt'n*	1001	tusen og en ***toos**sen oh ain*
1	en, ett *en, ett*	18	atten *att'n*	1 100	ett tusen ett hundre *ett **toos**sen ett **hoon**drer*
2	to *too*	19	nitten *nitt'n*	10 000	ti tusen *tee **toos**sen*
3	tre *tray*	20	tjue/tyve ***shoo**-er*	100 000	hundre tusen ***hoon**drer **toos**sen*
4	fire ***feer**er*	21	tjueen *shoo-er **ain***	1 000 000	en million *ain mil-**yoon***
5	fem *fem*	22	tjueto *shoo-er **too***		
6	seks *sex*	30	tretti/tredve ***tret**-ty*		1983 nitten åttitre 2005 to trusen og fem
7	sju/syv *shoo*	40	førti *furty*		(N.B. Nor. 6 : 3 = Eng. 6 ÷ 3 = 2) Nor. 9 ÷ 3 = Eng. 9–3 = 6
8	åtte ***ot**-ter*	50	femti *femty*		
9	ni *nee*	60	seksti *sexty*	1st	første ***furst**er*
10	ti *tee*	70	sytti ***sut**-ty*	2nd	andre ***and**rer*
11	elleve ***elv**er*	80	åtti ***ot**-ty*	3rd	tredje ***traid**-yer*
12	tolv *tol*	90	nitti ***nit**-ty*	4th	fjerde *f-**yair**er*
13	tretten *trett'n*	100	(ett) hundre *(ett) **hoon**drer*	5th	femte ***fem**ter*
14	fjorten *f-**yort**'n*	101	hundreogen ***hoon**drer oh ain*	6th	sjette ***shet**-ter*
15	femten *femt'n*	200	to hundre *too **hoon**drer*	7th	sjuende ***shoo**er-na*
16	seksten *sayst'n*	1000	(ett) tusen *(ett) **toos**sen*	8th	åttende ***otter**-na*